Yusuf Baba Gar

Capturing Culture

African Languages – African Literatures
Langues Africaines – Littératures Africaines

Volume 9

LIT

Yusuf Baba Gar

Capturing Culture

Traditional Theater
in Contemporary Hausa Video Films

LIT

Bibliographic information published by the Deutsche Nationalbibliothek
The Deutsche Nationalbibliothek lists this publication in the Deutsche
Nationalbibliografie; detailed bibliographic data are available in the Internet at
http://dnb.dnb.de.

ISBN 978-3-643-91410-1 (pb)
ISBN 978-3-643-96410-6 (PDF)

A catalogue record for this book is available from the British Library.

© LIT VERLAG GmbH & Co. KG Wien,
Zweigniederlassung Zürich 2022
Flössergasse 10
CH-8001 Zürich
Tel. +41 (0) 76-632 84 35
E-Mail: zuerich@lit-verlag.ch   https://www.lit-verlag.ch
Distribution:
In the UK: Global Book Marketing, e-mail: mo@centralbooks.com
In North America: Independent Publishers Group, e-mail: orders@ipgbook.com
In Germany: LIT Verlag Fresnostr. 2, D-48159 Münster
Tel. +49 (0) 2 51-620 32 22, Fax +49 (0) 2 51-922 60 99, e-mail: vertrieb@lit-verlag.de

This book is dedicated to my parents, wife and children

Table of Contents

ACKNOWLEDGEMENTS..9

1 Introduction - The Labeling Kannywood and Concept in Nigeria. 13

Transformation of Hausa Conventional Performances.........................17

2 The Hausa Kannywood Film Industry...19

On the Question of Cultural Imperialism..23

Towards a Liberal Approach to Kannywood Video Films...................25

The Further Side of Kannywood Video Films...................................33

3 Filming Folktales and Traditional Theatre 37

Filmic Shifts on Folk Narrative Contents...43

Adaptation as Valuable Resource in Filming 46

Adaptation and the Question of Fidelity...51

Adaptation as a Model of Transformation..54

Conclusion..60

4 Hausa Performing Arts in Contemporary Social Life...................63

Historical Background of the Hausa People......................................63

Oral Performances for Religious Purposes.......................................65

Oral Performance for the Aristocrats..74

Court Singers...75

5 From Performance to Theatre and to Video Films......................77

Hausa Modern Theatre Tradition to Film Medium............................80

The Impact of School Stage Drama on Film Production 81

Stage Theatre to Television Drama..81

Theatre and Film Production..83

Conclusion..84

6 Memory and Performance in Kannywood Films..............................**87**

Folktale Video Film: Ruwan Bagaja (Water for Cure)......................87

Folktale across Different Media...88

Analysis of Sangaya (2000) (Sangaya)..100

Elements of Metamorphosis of Status...100

Transition From Abstract Images to Physical Events.......................101

Ancient Practice Performance Video Film: Borin Ibro (2008)...........113

Analysis of Tashe (2010)..119

Performative Action Video Film: Fulani (2012)..............................127

Shift in Composition and Transmission of Verbal Utterances...........133

Analysis of Karen Bana (2013) 138

Conflation of a New Form of Media and the Oral Mode 139

Conclusion...151

7 General Conclusions..**153**

Filmography..**157**

Bibliography..**159**

ACKNOWLEDGEMENTS

First, I must acknowledge Prof. Dr. Susanne Gehrmann whose academic support has encouraged and motivated me. She gave me purposeful comments and criticisms. She is a model of benevolence.

Many thanks go to Dr. Joseph McIntyre. I benefited from his knowledge of Hausa and his popularity in Kano, Nigeria. He introduced me to Professor Abdalla Uba Adamu and Ado Ahmed Gidan Dabino from whom I got practical guidance

Prof. Dr. Abdalla Uba Adamu, the Vice Chancellor of National Open University of Nigeria (NOUN) deserves a special space in this book. Prof. Adamu received me at Kano, Nigeria wholeheartedly and then introduced me to Ahmad Salihu Alkanawy, Director and Member, Kano State Censorship Board with whom I worked throughout my fieldwork in Nigeria. In spite of his schedules, Prof. Adamu took the time to read the draft of this book and offered me useful comments and criticisms.

Professor Aderemi Raji-Oyelade, University of Ibadan, Nigeria and Professor Sule Emmanuel Egya, Ibrahim Badamasi Babangida University, Lapai, Nigeria deserve acknowledgments because their scholarly guidance propelled, instigated and inspired me.

I also wish to extend my profound gratitude and thanks to Professor Andrew Haruna, the Vice Chancellor, Federal University, Gashua, Nigeria along with his wife, Dr. (Mrs) Elizabeth Andrew, Department of Physical and Health Education, University of Jos, Nigeria. I did not only gain from Professor Haruna's encouragement, but I also benefited from his intensive, persistent and professional assistance over the years. I appreciate the kind of reception he offered me whenever I approached him for academic mentoring.

I would like to show my sincere thanks to Dr. Pepetual Mforbe Chiangong, who has constantly and willingly afforded me her time not only to read the drafts of this book, but also to make some comments. The same goes to Dr. Annekie Joubert, who encouraged me persistently through her question: When is the book going to be ready? Similarly, I remain grateful to Professor Ineke Phaf-Rheinberger for taking her time to walk into Room 401 to give me meaningful comments. Furthermore, I appreciate the encouragement from Dr. Lutz Diegner, Dr. Christfried Naumann, Dr. Chanfi Ahmed, Dr. Umma Aliyu Musa, Dr. Ari Awagana, Stefan Hoffmann and Mohammed Muhsin Ibrahim. To Obala Musumba, I say thank you for reading the draft of this book.

I must acknowledge Ahmad Salihu Alkanawy. I thank him for introducing me to all the filmmakers, actors and actresses whom I have interviewed in Kano and Kaduna. He has been a resourceful person, helpful and considerable on the issues surrounding Kannywood industry. I am grateful.

I also want to thank a host of academic professors who offered me time, advice and encouragement: Professor Dr. Tom Güldemann, Department of Linguistics, School of African Studies, Humboldt University Berlin; Professor Dr. Baz Lecocq, Department of History, School of African Studies, Humboldt University Berlin, Professor Herbert Igbonuasi, Department of Languages and Linguistics, University of Ibadan, Nigeria; Professor (Mrs) Asabe Kabir Usman, Department of Modern European Languages and Linguistics; Usman Danfodiyo University, Sokoto, Nigeria; and Professor James Tar Tsaaior, Department of Mass Media and Writing, Pan-Atlantic University, Lagos, Nigeria. Others are scholars in the Department of Languages and Linguistics, University of Maiduguri such as, Professor Munkaila Muhammad, Professor Ahmad Tela Baba, Professor Bassey Anthia, Professor Mohammed Aminu Muazu, Professor Balarabe Zulyadaini, Professor (Mrs) Aishatu Iya Ahmed, and Dr. Baba Mai Bello.

I am grateful to Humboldt University Berlin for sponsoring my trips to Nigeria for field research, without which this book wouldn't have been accomplished. I am most grateful to Astrid Kiesewetter and Josephine Karge, the Administration Staff of the Department of African Studies, Humboldt University Berlin. The same goes to all the Hausa students in my class as well as the entire members of the Colloquium on African Literature and Culture, whose comments have been the source of my confidence.

To Roman Büttner alias Malam Rabi'u, my German friend in Berlin, I am grateful for being accessible in both time of recreation and academics. Thank you so much to Harkanas Haruna, Sheikh Ubale Abdu and their families. I am grateful for the telephone calls that enhanced my great enthusiasm. Thank you to Joab Saje Kumo and his wife, Portia Joab, I am extremely grateful for being by me always. You have proved that a friend who will help someone when help is needed is a true friend.

I would like to mention members of my family to whom I owe a debt of appreciation. My wife Saratu Yusuf has been very supportive towards my academic career. She waited for quite a long time without me around her. She has been patient even at the time she needed me most. She has shown a unique woman's devotion to the progress of her family. She deserves a very special thank you. To Grace Yusuf Baba, Gloria Yusuf Baba, Gladys Yusuf Baba and Gift Yusuf Baba – my children - I say thank you for enduring daddy's absence for a long time. To Dinatu Yusuf, I also say thank you. In addition, I appreciate the support from Adamu Baba Gar, John Shehu Gar, Lydia Shehu Gar, Aminu Musa Filiya, Martha Aminu Musa, Ali Bello, Hannatu Ali Bello, Ephraim Jumba Gar, Ruth Ephraim Jumba, Kayinu Baba Gar and Rabi'u Jumba and the Management and staff of Abubakar Tatari Ali Polytechnic, Bauchi, Nigeria.

Finally, I admit that time and space will not permit me to mention all the stakeholders of this book. I do not only appreciate their contributions to the book, but I also consider its completion as our collective success.

1 Introduction - The Labeling Kannywood and Concept in Nigeria

This book looks at the way cultural memory of a traditional society in Africa is inserted into contemporary narratives of film production as mechanism of preservation of both theater performances and cultural heritage. Its specific field site focus is the Hausa video film industry of northern Nigeria, labeled "Kannywood" to distinguish it from the more common, English-language based Nigerian and globally known "Nollywood" film industry.

It analyzes five video films with inserted traditional cultural theater performances that are targeted at keeping alive a fading tradition of theater performance in the face of globalization of African orality and the disappearance of traditional African theater. The films analyzed, all in the Hausa language, were into performance based video films made in Northern Nigeria, dealing with artists involving narration to an audience. The state of Hausa orality is examined, the present status is assessed and evaluated. This is followed by a thorough analysis of selected performance video films such as Ruwan Bagaja (1998), Borin Ibro (2008), Tashe (2010), Sangaya (2000), Karen Bana (2013) and Fulani (2012). This analysis is based on the assessment of the situation, and my research considers shift and transformation as suitable terms to describe the state of the performances in the video films, especially now that technology is at its peak. With the introduction of electronics, people go for modern means of entertainment and the subsequent impact is that the oral performance of cultural art starts to change. Some Kannywood filmmakers are conscious of the fact that video films have become the impetus of not only entertainment, but also dissemination of information. Therefore, they transport traditional forms of performance into their video films. Their efforts might not necessarily be intended to bring the performances back to the village squares for people to practice them. Rather, transporting the performances into video films will enable people to be aware of their existence and social functions. It will also afford people the opportunity to know that this is their tradition and their culture. Kannywood filmmakers commit themselves to various types of video films. The inclusion of Hausa folktales and other performances such as tashe, bori and dambe in video films is due to their cultural acceptance based on the social and moral values they manifest. Being customarily and traditionally motivated, the filmmakers resort to those performances as symbols and resources of tradition, thus bringing viewers back to their heritage of oral literature.

However, considering the interviews which I conducted with directors during my field studies in Kano, most of them show that the manner in which the performances are transported into selected video films is by no means a process of just preserving the performances. While the filmmakers may think of preservation, this research considers the use of performance in video films as a development reflective of not only a transition but also the flexibility of culture to viewers, both at home and in the diaspora. However, in doing so, they also confirm that the immediate oral performance is not the only style to bring verbal art across anymore as observed by Furniss (1996:11): "Long gone are the days when the only way of seeing and hearing a verbal art performance was by being physically present as the story was told, the song was sung, or the play enacted".

This claim implies that the space and the medial support for orality are shifting. It purports that nowadays, live storytelling to children at home and live performances in village squares or market arenas are seldom seen. Alternatively, one discovers that some of these performances are shifted to screens of television for viewing at home. Filmmakers consider how the attention of children and the general public is moving towards motion pictures in addition to the availability of modern equipment. Therefore, they resort to folktales and other oral performances as source of storylines in order to influence people''s attention to their old narratives. If this realization is formative, then it will help in questioning the notion which suggests that Kannywood filmmakers tend to skip Hausa culture in their quest for filmmaking. As a first reference for example, Umar Faruk Asarani a viewer in Adamu (2007:64) crusades against cultural imperialism as he reacts to Kannywood video films in a letter to the Editor of Fim magazine. With regards to the intrusion of foreign values into Hausa culture through Kannywood video films Asarani thus writes,

I want to advice Nigerian Hausa film producers that using European music in Hausa film is contrary to portrayal of Hausa culture in films (videos). I am appealing to them (producers) to change their style. It is annoying to see a Hausa film with a European music soundtrack. Don't the Hausa have their own (music)? [....] The Hausa has more musical instruments than any group in this country, so why can't films be produced using Hausa traditional music?

Secondly, many people voiced concerns about the role of song and dance scenes (usually between an actor and actress in a garden) which dominate the plotlines of Kannywood video films. There is the fear that these video films are instructing viewers particularly the youths in the ways of romance instead of guiding them towards the themes of the storylines. A tension between the filmmakers and the Censorship Board in Kano emerges based on the repeated insertion of song and dance in Kannywood films. The Censorship Board opposes the insertion strongly, as the insertion enhances the interaction between boys and girls. Fim Magazine shows the drastic action taken by the Censorship as the September 2001 edition p. 59 reports in Hausa that,

An hana rawa da waƙa a finafinan Hausa
A cikin wata sanarwar bazata, gwamnatin jihar Kano ta soke rawa da kuma waƙe-waƙe a cikin finafinan Hausa wadanda ake shiryawa a cikin jihar.

Translation

Song and dance is banned in Hausa video films

In an unexpected announcement, the Kano State government have banned song and dance in Hausa video films which are produced in the state.

In the same Fim Magazine above, a viewer known as Muhammadu welcomes the decision on the ban and says "ya yi daidai" (it is correct) three times because for him, song and dance in the film is not useful. The subsequent chapter on the analysis of some selected Kannywood video films aim to tackle this major question.

More often than not, critics are more conscious of the influx of new traditions, but are seldom aware of how traditions fade away, whenever cultural changes are encountered. The affected societies usually forget that they are themselves the custodians of their culture and tradition. In addition, any culture that does not allow change suggests a societal stagnation. Modern societies allow themselves to lose hold and see their culture transformed. Rather than sticking to traditional and conservative ways, people should do everything humanly possible to embrace change with enthusiasm. Some Kannywood filmmakers work in that line. They remain culturally alert to consider the aesthetics of performances at the verge of extinction. Evidently, when filmmakers make use of material culture and oral practices in video films, it is like bringing performance back as a different practice, through a different media and people will be aware of this.

In Nigeria, the culture of labeling is a common phenomenon. In the field of written literature, the pamphlets-like prose fiction in the south of Nigeria, which are mostly displayed for sale in Onitsha, a renowned commercial city, are labeled Onitsha Market Literature. Their counterparts in the north, which are particularly widespread in Kano, also a commercial city, are identified as, Adabin Kasuwar Kano[1] (Kano Market Literature). Both the Onitsha Market Literature and the Kano Market Literature have received a mixture of reactions from the public, particularly the academics. These pamphlets are not only considered substandard, but they are also characterized with cases of violation of standard orthography and indecent expressions (Malumfashi, 2013:18). Abdalla Uba Adamu compiled the criticisms of the Kano Market Literature and titled it Annotated Bibliography of Criticisms Against Hausa Prose Fiction and posted it on Saturday, March 17, 2007.

While American films are linked with the label Hollywood, Indian films go by the label, Bollywood. In Nigeria, films in English which are produced in Nigeria by Nigerians are dubbed Nollywood. The Hausa video films that are produced in the north, with the main hub of production being Kano, are labeled, Kannywood, as indicated earlier. Therefore, Kannywood video films can be broadly conceptualized as

---

1   A term coined by Ibrahim Malumfashi to refer to a genre of Hausa novels (new prose fiction) which emerged in the early 1980s, precisely 1983 and 1984. The preeminent subject in the novels is *soyayya* (love, romance) thus, the novels are labeled *soyayya* novels. Mostly youths of below the ages of 25 were the principal participants in the processes of both writing and reading the novels. The youths were able to partake in the emergence of this genre due to the acquisition of writing and reading skills they have benefited from the Universal Primary Education scheme, which was launched in 1976 as a rapid campaign in a massive scale that witnessed the dawn of an educational revolution in northern Nigeria.

video films in Hausa produced in Nigeria, however, with close reference to northern Nigeria where Hausa is spoken. Although Nollywood happens to be a more noticeable Nigerian video film industry in the academic field and international circles, Abdalla Uba Adamu points out that the label "Kannywood" is a bit older than "Nollywood". He stated that the term emerged in 1999 in a Hausa-language magazine, Tauraruwa (Star) and was coined by Sunusi Shehu, the editor of the magazine who was also a Hausa-language novelist. This was three years before the name "Nollywood" was given to the Nigerian film industry in English by the New York Times in an article dated September 16, 2001 (Adamu, 2013:16).

Transformation of Hausa Conventional Performances

Change in culture and literature in general is becoming a necessary conversion due to social assimilation. It is leading a decisive step towards a shift to modernity. On the one hand shift results to distortions of traditional values, on the other hand adherence to traditional values is a setback to modernity. In any case, human beings are bound to exist at the same time or in the same place, taking advantage of fantasy and reality, not complacent or unconcerned about serious situations dealing with contemporary ideas. The aftermath of such coexistence, consciously or unconsciously involves existing beliefs being fused slowly with modernity through cultural appropriation, and more often than not, the loss or distortion of some traditional cultural elements ensues. In line with this, it is not unlikely to find an array of juxtapositions of conventional and modern cultures. This development enables societies to reconstitute themselves on different bases, bringing new identities and innovations to the forefront, maintaining cohesion as well. The new ideas that are established can become a basis for mobilization and transformation of the societies.

For instance, the culture of storytelling involving typical patterns of Hausa life is a changing space. It is hardly done anymore, except for some sketches among rural dwellers. However, it worth the challenge getting back to such norms or to indulge in the conventional genres of the tale that is oral fiction, which has been used as a means of moral lessons. If filmmakers use these sources in a mimetic way along with proper language style and costume, viewers have the chance to see them on screen. However, such performances are now gradually influenced by other cultural productions, in particular those to which Adamu (2007:16) refers as istanci (derived from Rupert East, the 'father' of modern Hausa prose fiction), a reference to the type of influence of Rupert East in virtually forcing the early Hausa prose fiction writers, specifically Abubakar Imam (1911-1981) to appropriate and domestically adapt foreign stories from Asia, the Middle East and Europe, especially in "Magana Jari Ce" (1938,Speaking is an Asset". It was a sheer semantic coincidence that Rupert East's name coincided with whole scale appropriation of Eastern form of literary cultures and entertainment by the Hausa in their performances, both in literature and film. The term "Istanci" (Eastism, as it were) was labeled to these appropriations by Hausaist scholar Nicolai Dobronravine of St. Petersburg (2003), even though the word has a niche in the English language as a scrabble game variant.

Adamu's concept includes both Islamic eastern and other eastern such as Indian non-Islamic cultural influences, particularly the Bollywood films. The benefit of using performances in video films is that they make cultural transitions evident. As children many of the filmmakers partook in oral performance as audience observers. These performances are thus part of their cultural memory. Today, when viewers see performances in video films, the performances can be considered as old wine in a new bottle. Film producers and directors use their time to produce fiction video films related to tradition and custom.

Although video films contain some cultural changes, by implication, they serve as memory of cultural performances. It is a big challenge to filmmakers because no matter the level of interest a filmmaker has in cultural films, this study considers that what viewers may see in the video films in this era of globalization will contain elements of cultural transformations and shifts. To justify this proposition, some video films are selected for analysis. The corpus of video films includes examples for different types of performances and different ways to integrate them in a film plotline. The selection along with the analysis is to unfold some of the sources of Kannywood video films and highlight some of the changes of performances that are encountered as they move from the oral public space to the medial space of video film.

2 THE HAUSA KANNYWOOD FILM INDUSTRY

This chapter provides an overview of the recent development of the Hausa video film industry in northern Nigeria by focusing on debates on culture and representation which characterize public discourse on the films in predominantly Muslim northern Nigeria. The Hausa video film industry, as opposed to the general Nigerian Nollywood film industry, attracted less attention from film researchers, perhaps due to its linguistic specificity that locates it within a particular social culture.

While a major part of the literature further claims that the imitation of foreign cultures by Kannywood filmmakers results in cultural imperialism and undermines religious motifs via insidious means; other critics dwell on the evolutionary background of the films, highlighting issues of secrets and revelations surrounding the Kannywood industry. At a more literary level, language strategies as employed by the filmmakers in respect to social behavior as a way of defining cultural identity of the society has been the interest of some researchers.

The literature claims that Kannywood's dependency on foreign media results into cultural imperialism. Adamu (2007) examines the impact of global trends and flows of popular culture on Muslim Hausaland from 1935 to 2005 in prose fiction, oral performing arts and video film. Adamu stresses that the process of globalization results in the emergence of the Hausa video film in 1990. According to Adamu, the video films are almost exclusively based on Hindi films. He states categorically that Hausa video films evolved around three main characteristics, "all borrowed heavily and inspired by Hindi cinema" Adamu (2007:47). He argues that Hausa films maintain Hindi film's style of plotlines and other basic characteristics such as love triangle, forced married, long song and dance scenes that aim mainly at the sexuality of the actresses. Although, in Adamu's opinion, these acts can be considered as means of modernizing Hausa culture, he nonetheless reiterates that they were not left unchecked, as they were counteracted by reactions from the religious fundamentalists and traditionalists. Adamu cites examples of points of clashes between transnational film techniques employed by Kannywood filmmakers and the fundamentalists/traditionalists. He further mentions scenes reserved for adult viewers like in Alhaki Kwikwiyo (2011) (Sin is a Puppy), Saliha? (1999) (Pious Woman?) and Malam

Karkata (1999) (The Fraudulent Cleric), stating that such films have received critical reactions from viewers as a result of their sexual connotations. In Adamu's opinion video films of these type and others that manifest "immoral acts", such as portraying Muslim-Hausa speaking actresses in skimpy dresses is viewed as intentionally chosen to seduce young male viewers. Such scenes have again provoked criticisms from viewers or those who uphold conservative traditional views when it comes to questions of morality. While this research upholds Adamu's opinion that Kannywood can be considered as a means of modernizing Hausa culture, it goes further to see the video films as popular culture that help in revitalizing the popular nature of Hausa culture.

Larkin (2000) discusses the influence of foreign media on Kannywood by looking at the rise of Hausa video within the wider sociology of what he describes as a "cassette or video culture" (2000: 210). Larkin explains how in the last two decades the emergence of video technology has transformed the Nigerian middle class and improved the availability of a massive range of the world's media products to those who can afford them (2000:209). According to him, transnational circulation of Indian films has offered Hausa videos an imaginative space where they might consider alternatives to both Western modernity and Hausa tradition. Video culture in the contemporary public sphere, as Larkin maintains, can be categorized into three discrete historical periods: the colonial era, the time of early independence up till the oil boom, and the post-oil boom era (2000:213). Since foreign films were commonly viewed at cinemas in major towns in northern Nigeria, Larkin argues that this phenomenon has given rise to a film culture in northern Nigeria. He states that in Kano alone, Indian films were shown five nights a week at the cinemas and one night each for Hollywood and Chinese films. This manifested into cultural borrowing just as Indian filmmakers also borrow from Hollywood as Larkin (2000:233) states:

The same is true of African popular culture, which has long been involved in acts of creative creolization where cultural influences from the West, the Islamic world, and Asia have been incorporated into African expressive traditions and their representational power subordinated to an African aesthetic.

He contends further that the most popular program on television was the Sunday morning Indian film on City Television (CTV), Kano; and most video shops reserved the bulk of their space for Indian films. According to

Larkin, the availability and easier access to Indian films make them so popular among Hausa viewers. One striking outcome of the influence of Indian cinema on the Hausa social life is through the medium of Hausa Rubutattun Littattafan Soyayya (Written Romance Stories), which were later coined as Adabin Kasuwar Kano (Kano Market Literature). Linking Kannywood video films to romantic fiction, Larkin asserts that Hausa viewers managed to engage with texts that show a culture that was "just like" Hausa culture while at the same time it was also different. It is no surprise that when the difference collapsed through the rise of littattafan soyayya (romantic fiction novels) Indian films became controversial in a way they never were before. However, Adamu (2007:89, 2010:70) recount how "some viewers of Kannywood video films have come to realize that it is the producers and the directors that are responsible for the corruption of culture and religion in Kannywood video films".

By inference, in addition to authors of these romantic fiction novels, the producers and directors of Kannywood video films too spread the modern love of Indian films to Hausa youths. The Indian films they watch are secondary because due to the film language Hindi, viewers usually do not understand what those films are about in detail, until the authors of Littattafan Soyayya, the producers and directors of Kannywood video films transport the contents into Hausa. This research takes into cognizance that globalization enhances the circulation of popular culture. Therefore, it is normal for cultures to be influenced by other cultures. This kind of cultural assimilation enables African culture to be flexible. The flexibility shows that culture is dynamic hence the human society has always been characterized by continuity and change.

Larkin (2002) further discusses the impact of Indian films on Hausa popular culture. He states how Indian films and the films' actors and music have been a dominant marker in popular culture in northern Nigeria. According to him, the desire for Indian films accounts for the adornment of the walls of tailor's shop and the windscreens of commercial buses with posters of Indian films stars. This development, Larkin argues, allows Indian films to have access into the dialogue construction of Hausa popular culture by giving Hausa men and women an alternative world similar to their own. However, Larkin wonders what pleasures do Hausa viewers derive from watching films that portray a different culture and religion from theirs, especially as the dialogues are in a language they might not be able to decode. My research serves as useful reminder that social systems are dynamic and are often influenced by other cultures especially when it comes to cultural productions and the media of expression. More so, one of the functions of film is entertainment and as film comprises both language and action, viewers are likely to understand the film from the actions involved without necessarily understanding the language. In addition, the constant repetitive cast of characters whose roles are restricted within the borders of behaviors of the father, the mother and the wicked antagonist provides an easy understanding and makes translation of video film possible despite cultural and linguistic differences. Another example which proves this is the popularity of Nollywood, Nigerian films in English among viewers in Francophone African countries.

Adamu (2010) elaborates on the conflict between filmmakers and Islamic religious sects, and the step taken by the Censorship Board to regulate the emerging threat and raising chaotic settings and their effects on culture and the society at large. Adamu (2010: 63) explains that, "Hausa films as new medium, are a source of conflict in northern Nigeria, due to the films' representation of the Hausa Muslim woman's private space". Adamu maintains that in pre-colonial Hausa culture, folktale which was part of Hausa popular culture mainly focused on aspects of Hausa life that have to do with upholding moral standards. Sexuality, according to Adamu, was a taboo subject in pre-colonial Hausa popular cultural productions (2000:64). Shifting from folktale to visual media, Adamu indicates that television drama reinforced the traditional arrangement of the Hausa spatial structure because no bedroom scenes were foregrounded. Further, he argues that the problem came with the transition from television drama to video films that were influenced by Hindi and American cinematic styles in which the Muslim Hausa female sacred space was exposed. According to Adamu, the films revolves around family crisis and how to overcome them rather than relying on local folktales. Thus, the development in Hindi cinema in the 1990s has influenced Hausa filmmakers after 2000 in ways that the latter adopted patterns similar to Indian song, dance and choreography in their films, a further move revealed the exposure of female private space. As a result of this, Hausa video filmmakers were accused of contemptuously disregarding the Hausa culture. According to Adamu, this infringement of traditional norms of privacy in Hausa video films has made a dual impact.

First, it attracts criticisms and secondly, it uncovers the tension between globalization and Hausa Muslim culture (2010:72).

On the Question of Cultural Imperialism

Focusing on filmic discourse Chamo (2012) examines ways of interactions in Hausa film discourse, which according to him are seemingly contrary to the traditional norms of communication. Although his research is rooted in language studies, his views offer relevant information on the changes Hausa society undergoes in the area of social and cultural relations as reflected in Kannywood video films. Chamo assesses the films' discourse by examining the actors' and actresses' attitudes towards communicative performances such as contextually marked forms and language skills (related to the use of figurative expressions), attitude towards language and language varieties (code-switching and youth register) and attitude towards language choice and language use (forms of address and presence of new topics in public discourse). Chamo's main research question is: "to which extent is the language of the film changing and which group of the society is influenced with the new culture phenomenon?" (2012:27). In an attempt to arrive at a response to this question, Chamo examines the films' dialogues between boyfriend and girlfriend. Bearing in mind that in the traditional set up, boyfriend and girlfriend cannot converse while standing within public gaze, Chamo sees this traditional rule "totally broken" (2012:79) in Hausa films, where girls express their emotions directly to their boyfriends and show their love towards them. Therefore, according to Chamo, the discourses in Hausa video films are different from the traditional Hausa norms of communication and opposed to Hausa cultural values, signaling clearly that both Hausa language and culture are undergoing transformations in the contemporary world. Even though Chamo shows how the status quo of traditional rule is totally broken due to influence of new cultural phenomena, his work fails to consider other foreign influences on Hausa language when words and phrases from English, Arabic and some local languages in Nigeria appear in the video films' discourses. More often than not, there are scenes in some video films that show actors such as Dan Gwari, Baban Chinedo and Dan Yarbawa who imitate Gwari, Igbo and Yoruba. The linguistic flexibility therefore extends to cultural flexibility because language and culture are closely interwoven. In Larkin's observation, the wearing of Western-style clothes, the use of English by members of the upper-class or by government officials and growing materialism, which results in endemic corruption in the post-colonial state are some of the familiar situation viewers are taking part in (2002:22). In a similar vein, Ahmad observes the interfaces between traditional and modern life styles in Hausa society. According to him, any visitor to Kano or any city in northern Nigeria is bound to be amazed by an array of juxtapositions of traditional with modern cultures (2005:219) Based on this, the present research lays emphasis on Hausa culture's flexibility and refutes that it is broken.

Contrary to Chamo's language studies approach, McCain (2014) is more concerned with political issues: the conflict between conservative critics, and the bureaucrats over Hausa films. The critics' views, in McCain's opinion, are based on cultural pollution in northern Nigeria and how conflict has affected the Kannywood industry, resulting in the industry becoming almost extinct. McCain (2014:2) further states that, "Hausa artists are not really exposed on the national or the global stage thus paucity of knowledge on and about Hausa popular culture transpires". Although she acknowledges the multiple forms of transnational media flows into northern Nigeria, which according to her generate controversies about the films produced by Kannywood, she claims that exposure is a major problem.

One of such controversies which McCain speaks about is the exposure of the moral corruption within the Kannywood industry, particularly the sexual corruption of women by men or in some cases by each other. She explains that exposure of Kannywood actresses in relation to her work can be seen as a form of revelation, unmasking hidden spaces and the dirty underside of a "showy exterior" (2014:5). McCain contends that the idea of exposure was put into circulation by the Kano State Censorship Board and by other conservative critics to refer to the unmasking of the secret sins of corrupt members of Kannywood industry, fears about the over-exposure of young women in the industry and, finally, negative influences in which Kannywood video films were exposing to vulnerable viewers.

McCain finds out that exposure as it relates to Kannywood, therefore, is an idea that is used by all actors in the controversy. While filmmakers often claim they are exposing the corruption of the elites, censorship officials maintain that Kannywood films expose the immorality of the artists, whereas cultural elites use it to express their concern that Nigeria is being embarrassed on the global stage by making substandard productions. I find that McCain's (2014) study covers many important aspects. In dealing with the controversy surrounding Kannywood industry, the work exposes the three principal stakeholders.

Towards a Liberal Approach to Kannywood Video Films

Further culture clash in the Kannywood film perception is revealed by Muhammad (2002) who analyzed the perception of women in Kannywood films.. Muhammad agrees that there is interaction between actors and actresses in Hausa video films and it is this interaction that makes viewers think that the actresses do act in the same way beyond video film's interaction whenever they are outside video film's space. According to Muhammad, critics of Kannywood fail to acknowledge the video films as means of awareness and economic empowerment, neither do they consider why viewers embraced the films within a short period of time. She examines the roles women take in the films and finds out that, more often than not, they take the role of mothers. This role, according to Mohammed is very (necessary) important for filmic plotlines in general. On the other hand, they take the role of grandmothers or mother-in-laws who usually interfere in their sons' matrimonial issues to the detriment of their daughters-in-law, in order to send a strong message to those women who engage in such acts. Mohammed argues that the films can be considered as a means of correction. In an investigation, seventy percent of people prefer watching the films than listening to sermons because according to them, the films can be considered as sermon (2002:142).

In the same fashion as Muhammad (2002), Umar's (2002) differs from most works that center on criticisms. According to him, most critics of Kannywood video films misunderstand filmmaking. This shortcoming, Umar argues, makes the critics to think that there is nothing good in all Hausa films except cultural pollution. Umar believes that no script writer can pick up his pen and develop storylines with the intention of polluting his culture. According to him, if viewers can make a critical analysis of Hausa video films, they will understand that there are meaningful lessons in the video films, which are aimed towards reforming Hausa society.

More so, the video films contain Hausa genres such as proverbs, epithets and songs which are vital components of Hausa literature, Umar reiterates.

In their discussion of three Hausa video films, Idoko and Munkaila (2004) identified the place of the films in their local context, and seek to negotiate their place and relevance within the global space, thereby highlighting some of their important features. The authors go on to include an excursion into the history of the evolution of Hausa video films in Nigeria and then discuss the social and cultural necessities of the video films within the indigenous system and the global situation. They acknowledge the existence of theatre traditions among the Hausa and maintain that the video films could be said to be an extension of these dramatic activities in a different context, celebrating the socio-cultural relationships of the Hausa (2004:56). In their analysis of the three films the authors discuss the dominant structure of moral content that is inherent in Hausa video film. For example, the serious question about the morality of telling lies, intricacies of relationships and marriage, and the morality of good family relationship. Like most researchers, Idoko and Munkaila recognize the influence of Indian, Chinese and Western film traditions in Hausa video films by saying that:

It is understandable that the Hausa video films develop and produce specific cultural meanings through the medium and effect from Western/Eastern tool, and an attempt to have relevance in the world [....] it does not exclude its undercurrents of a negotiated place in the globalization trends, neither does it imply seeing or accepting the Western/Eastern frame of mind as synonymous with accepting or qualification to be termed as having a global acceptability, rather it sees culture (2004:62).

The arguments of Muhammed (2002), Umar (2002), Idoko and Munkaila (2004) can be used in this research to uphold the claim that there are Kannywood video films particularly the Sharia compliant video films that conform to and comply with the local cultural values.

The proceedings of the first international conference on Hausa films, organized by the Center for Hausa Cultural Studies, Kano and hosted by Bayero University, Kano, Nigeria, from 4th – 7th August, 2003 were published in 2004 as Hausa Video Films: Technology, Economy and Society, edited by Adamu, Adamu, and Jibril. Out of concern for a meaningful future of the Kannywood industry, Adamu acknowledges the lack of critical study of the relationship between media technologies and transformations in Hausa popular culture, especially at a time of increasing importance of media technology on popular culture; and how Hausa urban youths are redefining the pattern of entertainment in Hausa communities. While there are no significant local inputs that show the relationship between Hausa culture and popular culture as a vehicle of cultural preservation and transmission, Adamu notes that the most significant advances in this area were carried out by foreign researchers, the outcome of which Adamu says, "is considered an authoritative account of the acculturation of the Indian culture on Hausa home video industry" (2004:3).

Krings (2004) points out an outstanding comparison which touches both similarities and differences between wasan bori (spirit possession play) and video dramas in Hausa. Krings states that both are modes of performing arts in northern Nigeria. He argues that both wasan bori and video dramas in Hausa have a common base: the two are connected to theatre. In the comparison, he shows that wasan bori and video dramas share two similar fields of social interaction because both wasan bori and video dramas are closely akin to theatre by containing a free mixture of both sexes. Krings asserts further that by their relation to theatre both wasan bori and video dramas allow their participants to exhibit a relatively partial appropriation of otherness, meaning that the actors and actresses are representing something or someone else, and not themselves while performing on the dance ground or acting on the screen (2004:163). On the differences, Krings posits that there seems to be class difference between the participants of wasan bori and video dramas. While wasan bori absorbs the illiterates or those with only a few years of primary education, video dramas, especially the actors and viewers are linked or associated with the literates. This study finds Krings article interesting because it uncovers the ignorance of some critics of Kannywood video films who argue against actors and actresses coming together, for example, Mahmud (2008). Unless the critics are hypocrites and have prejudice, they should not have been subjective in their approaches to Kannywood. They ought to have known about bori, which Krings refers as a social interaction in Hausa culture that is characterized by a free mixture of males and females. By implication, this interaction is now extended to Kannywood industry.

Mohammed centers on women's public gaze and acting, particularly in northern Nigeria. Mohammed gives a definition of women on screen as "performing women", such as actresses, musicians, newscasters, etc. (2004:194). However, she focuses on actresses in Hausa video films. Mohammed's attention is drawn by the criticisms and debate in northern Nigeria on Muslim Hausa women and acting in Kannywood video films. In her defense of acting women, Mohammed ascribes to the importance of casting actresses in video film and argues that women are more suitable in certain roles, and when they pick up such roles, viewers enjoy watching video films. For this reason, Mohammed maintains that the need for actresses came up since the emergence of Hausa video films. In line with the notion "actress stands for prostitute" (2004:196) among some viewers in Hausa society, Mohammed conducted interviews and the result of her findings is that eighty percent of men in the film industry can marry an actress if she fulfills certain moral and social conditions such as being respectful, educated, decent, and of good family background. These conditions are generally demanded from none actresses as well. Outside the industry, 80 percent of men said they cannot marry an actress on any condition and twenty percent agree to marry an actress if she will quit acting. Mohammed argues that the industry is full of decent actresses. Therefore, she recommends that viewers should see acting as a play, out of the playwright's imagination whose sole aim is to send a message across. Therefore, the concept that actresses are prostitutes should be discouraged. She encourages the public to regard an actress as any normal woman whose behavior on the screen was only for a reason and it is temporal. This dissertation finds Mohammed's work very objective, as it has neither grudge nor prejudice. Based on my interviews, the actresses confess that they seek the approval of their parents before engaging as actress. Can parents allow their daughters to participate in filmmaking if it were for prostitutes and notorious girls?

Maikaba (2004) examines the influence of foreign cinema on contemporary Hausa home video drama. He discusses the reasons for the adoption of Indian cultures in the production of Hausa home video drama. He states that the Hausa people of northern Nigeria have been used to Indian films for over half a century. In order to bring these viewers close to them, Maikaba insists that Kannywood filmmakers need to create something close to the aesthetics of Indian films viewers were used to. Another basis for the adoption of foreign culture in Hausa home video drama, according to Maikaba, was the absence of indigenous entertainment media for Hausa youths. On the same vein, the influence of foreign cinema on Hausa home video and culture could be viewed from the doses of American / British films shown on local television stations in northern Nigeria for years. He argues that popular American / British films have been on our screens for over two decades. (2004:104). Maikaba recommends the inception of a new acceptable format for Hausa home video drama which may be reflective of Hausa culture and traditions. In Maikaba's opinion, this is the only way the Hausa could feel proud of their culture and promote its export to the outside world. However, to recommend an acceptable format for Hausa video films which can reflect on Hausa culture and tradition indicates that little does Maikaba know about those storylines in Kannywood video films which are based on oral tales. Indeed, my research highlights how orality is used by filmmakers as source of video films. This technique which the filmmakers have adopted is to incorporate modern technology in order to give the best possible expression of an indigenous genre. Basically, the knowledge of culture and technology by the filmmakers helps to actualize this strategy. By this research therefore, we can see how much film adapts to the multimedia and performance qualities of oral tradition and how much technical refinement gives it full expression.

While Maikaba is worried at the level of influence of foreign cultures on Kannywood video films, Ahmed's concern is focused on the reactions of Kano Ulama (Muslim Clerics) to Kannywood video films. Ahmed considers and discusses specifically, what the Muslim clerics object in the films, the basis for the objection and what they think should be done by producers to meet the basic religious requirements in their productions. In tackling this task, Ahmed discusses the position of drama, music and dance (three genres in Hausa video) in both Islam and Hausa conventional society. He posits that the concept of drama is an established concept in Islam, and it includes actual mimicking of certain acts in order to demonstrate or emphasize a point (2004:146). Similarly, in Hausa conventional society, according to Ahmed, drama is also a well-known phenomenon even before the advent of colonialism, and with modifications, some of these dramatic acts have continued to date. He refers to genres which are generally referred to as Wasannin Gargajiya (Traditional Performances). To Ahmed, the concept of drama and performances in Hausa society are well-established to warrant further justification. Besides that, he argues that some of these drama forms are recognized and accepted in Islam. Therefore, he maintains that drama as an element of Hausa film should not, generally speaking, attract any controversy. Even though Ahmed (2004) supports his arguments more on religious bases, this work finds Ahmed's opinions useful. As he ignores the dynamic cultural aspect and the role of globalization, the present work seeks to elaborate on these aspects.

Contrary to Ahmed above, Abdullahi takes the moralist's approach to question the principles or standards of good behavior in Hausa films and the system of censoring the video films. He identifies the types of acts in Hausa films that violate Islamic moral codes, which warrant criticisms from Muslim scholars and moralists. Some of the behaviors which he identifies as wrong because they disagree with what is generally accepted, especially with regard to religion and genuine Hausa culture in the video films, are singing and dancing by actor and actress, rampant cultural borrowing, advocating and encouraging idolatry in disguise and promoting breach of trust. Abdullahi investigates the causes of these social irregularities found in Kannywood video films and finds out that the first reason can be attributed to lack of professionalism in filmmaking by both the producers, actors and actresses. This shortcoming, according to Abdullahi predominate the filmmakers and influences particularly the producers thereby revolving the main theme of almost all the video films. Secondly, Abdullahi observes that there is the urge for wealth and quick fame by the filmmakers. As a result of this most of the filmmakers in the industry copy foreign cultures (American, Chinese and Indian). The present work does not aim at disputing Abdullahi's claim. Rather, it seeks to investigate if there are Kannywood video films that conform to and comply with cultural values. However, the question is: are there changes in the cultural values and what are the changes? This is a departure from Abdullahi's work, which makes blatant generalizations and disregards of the variety and complexity of Kannywood video films.

Maiwada examines the underlying trends in the development of Hausa video films. He discovers that in the video films there are emphases on violence, which according to him are clear examples of imitations of foreign films. To him, if violence should persist in Kannywood video films, definitely the films will bear negative consequences on the behavior of youths. Maiwada argues that Hausa video films imitate storylines of Hausa novels that themselves imitate Indian films which depict love, marriage and marital problems. According to Maiwada, these are contrary to the Hausa classical novels, which portray themes with focus on norms and values of Hausa-Islamic society. He insists that themes in classical Hausa novels ought to have continuity in Hausa video films. On the contrary, the pattern has shifted to the imitation of violence as portrayed in Indian or English films especially in the video films Sharaɗi (2002), Isaah (ND) and Uƙuba (2001). Maiwada asserts that these video films will have a negative effect on the behavior of children and youths engaged in viewing as evident in numerous studies conducted to demonstrate the impact of screen violence on children and youths (2004:273). Maiwada reemphasizes that children or even adolescents who are exposed to violent television shows over a period of time can demonstrate changes in their behavior. Based on this, he recommends the need to draw the attention of producers to turn to the rich contents in Hausa folklore and early Hausa novels for inspiration for their films. It seems that Maiwada is expecting Kannywood to be like an isolated entity which is supposed to operate in a self-contained manner. On the contrary, this work considers that in the space of work of art, many utterances and actions are taken from other works. When they are taken, they intersect and neutralize one another in form of cross-cultural influences.

Dakata, like other contributors to the publication, focuses on the penetration of certain foreign cultures into Hausa video films. Dakata discusses foreign influences on Hausa video films. According to him, the alien cultures are appearing to be genuine, whereas they are not. Dakata argues that the effect of embracing such foreign cultures by Kanwood filmmakers is resulting into worsening the alteration and alienation of the Hausa-Fulani culture (2004:250). Dakata observes that the influx of Indian films in Hausa society from the 80s to 90s has the highest influence on Hausa home video. He laments that instead of using "our culture to promote and sustain our indigenous development, we take to copying, and imitating Indians" (2004:251). He claims that gender relations among the youths in Hausa video films appear very alien. According to him, no right-thinking Hausa-Fulani parents would allow their daughter to go to parks or bushes to dance and sing with a boy. He cites the example of Harsashi (2003), a video that presents what he considers as "fashion defile" (2004:251) instead of "beauty contest" as indicated in the video film. To Dakata, the appearance of ten maidens in wedding gowns enticing a young man for friendship in the video is not only foreign, but seems to be just not feasible in Hausa society. He calls on the Hausa-Fulani, as Africans, to know what is good for them rather than adopting all foreign cultures wholeheartedly. To the artists in the film industry he says they must take it upon themselves or regard it as a point of duty to lead incoming artists in making efforts to correct these anomalies. While Dakata sees only the negative aspect of imitation, he fails to realize that imitation can be used in making reference to a pre-existent reality only. Therefore, my work considers it as a highlighting in which, by inclusion in video films, the actors and actresses do not always mean what we are doing is what should be done. They may be engaged in a process of expressing either belonging to or separation from the culture in question. Generally, another fact about imitation is that it has to do with materials known to the imitators because it is logical that one cannot imitate something he or she does not know about. In this sense, the actors and actresses in Kannywood video films have already known that song and dance exist in the culture, and their appearance in video films should not be a course of concern.

Mohammed takes a feminist direction. He laments at the way Hausa women remain reprimanded and oppressed. Mohammed relates to the above lamentation by investigating and analyzing the representation of Hausa women in Hausa video films. He focuses on the types of roles women play and the religious symbols being affected in the representations of women. Mohammed agrees that women have been given central roles in Hausa video films. However, he argues that, the roles they play represent a persistent view of women as having less importance than men. According to him, the video films represent them as unstable, destructive and absurd or without reasoning and understanding. More often than not, they are portrayed as the one responsible for broken homes. They can conspire among themselves or with men to execute deadly plots, and at the end they are made to pay the price of their negative acts by becoming dangerous lunatics, divorced and losing their lovers or their lives (2004:180). The portrayal of women as less important human beings or as subordinates in Hausa home video is seen in Sukuni (ND), a film in which a father keeps on persisting that his daughter should come up with a man whom she wants to marry, because as a daughter she has to produce a husband at a given time, if not she should be prepared and willing to accept any man chosen by her father. On the representation of women as destructive and evil in the video films, Mohammed cites Furuci (2001) as an example in which the character Hajiya single-handedly destroys two families including her own. Having discussed the stereotypes of women as represented in Hausa video films, Mohammed recommends the need for further research into the roles of women in various spheres of Hausa society such as cultural, economic, political and religious that will reflect progressive and community attitudes. My work strives to contribute to this necessity.

The Further Side of Kannywood Video Films

From most of the groundbreaking literature on Kanywood reviewed so far, emphasis deals largely with influence of Indian films and transnational media flows. The latter paradigm, the "transnational media flows" on the one hand, designates the growth of technology which facilitated digital and digitalization a day-to-day expression and altered the media environment in seemingly rudimentary ways. On the other hand, the new global space of flows enabled by the force of the media safeguards the interaction between technology and culture often referred to as technoculture. More commonly, the internet serves as a driving force and enhances trans-border flows. Evidently, production, circulation and consumption of various cultures are absolutely more feasible now.

Regarding the former paradigm, specifically, the literature shows how Bollywood films have had influence on Hausa viewers and how the films became the back bone of Kannywood video films, thereby enhancing 'cultural imperialism'. This work does not consider imitation as a matter of copying the preexistence material, but competing with it. Kannywood video films in this case compete with Indian films and most northern Nigerian viewers of Indian films come to embrace Kannywood video films for two main reasons. First, the actors and actresses are known to the viewers.

Second, the storylines in Kannywood video films are in Hausa. It seems viewers have come to terms with Larkin's question: What pleasures do Hausa viewers derive from watching Indian films especially as the dialogues are in Hindi, a language they are not able to decode (2002:21)? In a more concise view, this work considers Kannywood video films as a concerted effort of filmmakers who produce video films out of their personal experience, and those who try to improve society for the better. By doing so, the video films will help in demonstrating the common humanity in all cultures. As some stakeholders in the industry argue, the video films deal with the realities of day to day life and even their own experiences. In particular, Musa Abdullahi Sufi, an actor in an interview with me at Bagauda Hotel, Kano on September 7, 2011 says, "I believe every simple thing you see in Hausa movie is the reflection of what happens in the society."

The focus of this book, however, is not on the viewers of Kannywood video films, what they watch on screen and what they are really understanding from the films' narratives. Kannywood video films have various sources of storylines which are indigenous. These sources originate from Hausa reality and have an outstanding significance in Hausa culture. Such videos with indigenous background are on display side by side with those video films whose sources are from imported cinema. The exposure of this development might result into Kannywood video films receiving more acceptability for their ability to contain dual sources, both local and foreign, thus depicting cultural hybridity at the time of globalization. To achieve this, the work reflects beyond the existing two categories of Kannywood: Camama (cheap, often comedic skits and films made in less than a week) and Sentimental (elaborate features, mainly romantic), which are the commonly used categories known among filmmakers. However, the reflection on the categories is not intended to suggest camama and sentimental as the only two final categories. Rather, it is aimed at bringing to the limelight more Kannywood video films, some solely build on locale conventional performances, while others on foreign dimensions. This book sees Kannywood video films as popular culture that helps in reviving the popular nature of Hausa culture. In addition, selection and analysis of video films which include oral tradition shall be a major topic of discussion in this book. This is an area that has been overlooked by previous research on Kannywood video films.

The critics of Kannywood video films seem to claim that they are ardent supporters and promoters of Hausa culture which, according to them, Kannywood filmmakers fail to be. Today, the cinematic arts in Africa go beyond the issue of cultural imperialism. The presence of technology serves as a means of cultural out-reach, irrespective of which culture. Little do the critics know that some storylines in Kannywood video films are based on orality. My work highlights how orality is used by filmmakers as source of video film. This technique adopted by filmmakers is to incorporate modern technology in order to give the best possible expression of an African genre. The strategy comes basically from a cross-fertilization of oral knowledge, popular culture and technology. Therefore, in Kannywood, we see how much film can adapt to the multimedia and performance qualities of oral tradition and how much technical refinement can give it full expression. I conclude the review with the following quotations: "Nothing is said now that has not been said before" and "Would I had phrases that are not known, utterances that are not strange, in new language that has not been used, free from repetition, not an utterance which has grown stale, which men of old have spoken" (Juvan, 2008:13-14).These two quotations suggest that every work of art is a mention about another thing which has already at one time been mentioned, or its rejection. Specifically, this is the central idea that is contained in imitation. It denotes connection and mutual dependence of two component conditions.

The ideas in the above quotation are within the broader concept of intertextuality. The term intertextuality, according to Juvan (2008:11), was invented, defined and launched in semantic theory and literary studies by Julia Kristeva between 1966 and 1974. The inherent idea about intertextuality centers on not only the text as limitless, having no boundaries, but also on the fact that other texts and discourses intrude amid the printed lines. The idea suggests that nothing exists outside the text. However, the emergence of electronic media has entirely and thoroughly changed the nature of texts. Therefore, this work does not only find today's digital era broadening the initial scope of intertextuality, but it also transforms and encompasses other genres which dwell on everyday experience. Therefore, the key motivating factor is the notion among critics of Kannywood that the video films are an imitation of Indian films.

3 FILMING FOLKTALES AND TRADITIONAL THEATRE

This chapter focuses on transition from folktale and theatre to film. It is aimed at exploring how films are built on already existing medium, that is how films recycle folktale and theatre and then send them back to the performers of folktale and theatre in particular and viewers in general, thus manefisting the convergence of traditional folktale and theatre with contemporary filmic medium. Mikel J. Koven (2008:3) acknowledges the function of folklorists as avid collectors of contemporary legends and the task of films as users and dissiminators of contemporary legends. Invariably, filmmakers through folklorists have considerable skill to recognize and uncover the homogenizing cultural manifestations through the mass media especially video films.

On the one hand, attention is on the transfer of content involving mainly orality from one medium to another. The transfer of the folktale *Daskin Da Ridi* into video film of the same title is an evidence, as Ahmad (2004:154) states, "the adaptation of *Daskin Da Ridi* tale into a film by Sarauniya Production is worthy of emulation". As the case shows, Hausa folktales can function as a considerable source for scripting the storylines of Kanyywood video films. On the other hand, attention will also include discussion on the notion of adaptability of imaginative ideas, and their subsequent transformation into the new visual narrative medium, as remediation, which focuses on the inclusion or visual representation of one medium into another medium does not only mean the effortless lift of content. Prior to the transfer of the folktale *Daskin Da Ridi* into video film, the prose fiction of Abubakar Tafawa Balewa titled *Shaihu Umar* was converted into video film of the same tiltle by Adamu Halilu. And as a mark of interest in cinema studies and preservation of endangered materials that could be used for academic purposes, the Goethe University Frankfurt, Germany in collaboration with the Nigerian Film Corporation, Lagos along with the Film Society and Arsenal Berlin, Germany, Halilu's classic 1976 film of *Shaihu Umar* is currently involved in the process of restoration. This development suggests the fact that focus remains at looking at how some cultural elements, whether folktale or not, are modernized as part of collective memory in Kannywood video films.

The conventional folktales in general and Hausa folkates in particular are built on conventionalized human characters such as the favourite child, the wicked child, wicked step mother, animal and supernatural characters such as ghosts and witches. The animal characters, more often than not in metaphoric conviction, make transformation feasible, as animation has already demonstrated the workability of animal characterization in video films. Yahaya (1971) and Usman (2012) contain folktales such as *Gizo Da Budurwar Danko* and *Budurwa Marar Tabo* respectively. In these two folktales, both humans and animals feature as characters, a representation of traditional cultures with emphasis on monsters and belief in heritage of classical times. Once these types of folktales are used for video films, the films can be regarded as the modern illusory or imagenary stories of developed humankind due to the intersections and criss-crisings of folktale and popular film. In this regard, Koven (2008:4) confirms video films as both an astonishing medium of tale circulation and a kind of story-telling event. He points out how the animated cartoon is the most of all mediums that has achieved desired results for the presentation of the fairy tale. Indeed, Koven expresses that many adults who had long ago let go their attentiveness in the fairy tale in a way that is not expected, have afterwards found great delight in the old medium of the folk imagination. This is made possible in cooperation with new lightweight cameras and equipments which provided for filmmakers substantial adaptability, in addition to their willingness to change and innovate. Therefore, filmmakers are able to capture folktales of oral traditions exhaustively and then transmit the reality of these folktales on the screen to their viewers. For examples from Hollywood, refer to *Snow White and the Seven Dwarfs* (1937)[2] and *Cinderella* (2015 Disney Film)[3]

---

2   *Snow White and the Seven Dwarfs* was produced by Walt Disney Production in 1937. It is an American animated fantasy film based on the German fairy tale by the Brothers Grimm. It is regarded as the first full-length animated feature film as well as the earliest Disney animated feature film. The film was not only considered sufficiently outstanding or remarkable to be worthy of recognition historically, aesthetically and culturally, but it was also among the twenty five films chosen for preservation in the National Film registry in the USA. See https://en-.wikipedia.org/wiki/snow_white_and_the_seven_Dwarfs_(1937_film). Accessed on December 15, 2020.

3   *Cinderella* (2015) is a romantic fantasy film based on a folktale as well as Walt Disney's 1950 animated film. It is an exploration into segregation portrayed pointedly against a member of the same family. Ella, played by Lily James encounters difficulties, as severe punitive measures were meted out to her by her cruel stepmother and stepsisters. However, Ella finally experiences a turning point, as she comes into contact with a happy ending, which fits a typical fair tale hero's characteristics in most fairy tales. See

A video film on folktale no doubt is remediating orality since in the attempt to absorb the old medium, (folktale) insertion of images, sound and light into the mew medium (video film) is deliberated. Basically, such elements which are visible and are often referred to as visual remediation such as image and light make viewers aware of not only replacement of items in the new medium, but also the changes that are involved. Hence, the new medium justifies itself through remediating old medium. More often than not, folktale circulation in the video film would not only be discerned, but would also stimulate and champion viewers to rediscover the folktales. More importantly, one individual folktale in video film could get as far as many viewers at the same time. Sherman and Koven (2007:5) provide awareness into Egypt's vernacular cinema. The ways the films give a reversion of the traditional beliefs of the country is not only expressed, but also conveyed is the strong impact on Egyptian films of Hollywood narratives. The way the films evolve back into their own culture, suggests that their folktale is transformed by the popular culture of the West.

To give some few examples of folktale to movie adaptions from Hoolywood, let me first refer to *Thor* (2011) as evidence for or justification of my argument. The film is based on Thor, the Norse god of strength, thunder, war and storms according to Norse mythology. The tale was popular in Norway, Denmark and Sweden. Secondly, I refer to *Tangled* (2011) which is based on the German fairy tale "Repunzel" in the collection of folktales published by the Brothers Grimm. The film apprises an account of past events in the life of a lost, young princess. The princess hair is not only magical, but it is also long and blonde. She craves to go away from her concealed tower. Contrarary to or in opposition to her mother's inclination, she consents to the encouragement and assitance of an intruder to convey her into the world which she has not for a moment in her life seen. As typical of folktale, the film's characters include both humans with extra magical powers and animals who partake in some traits that are unique to humans.

The use of folktale as the foremost plotline or connecting subject matter for commercial feature films has become an evident factor that seek to transpire in films. This situation shows how filmmakers use folktales in their films. and how filmmakers are not only in unmediated

https://en.wikipedia.org/wiki/Cinderella_(2015_Disney_film). Accessed on December 15, 2020 exposure with folktales, but also, their interrelation with folk culture is more effortlessly demonstable. More often that not, linkage between the film and the legitimate folk culture does not enjoin one to consider whose relatedness is deemed to be reliable and authentic. Rather, identification of the source is more suitable. To this effect, (Koven 2008:10), identifies traditional tale-types and motifs in films and notes the similarities between Vietnam war movies and traditional narratives in books.

It could be right to say that in Kannywood video films as well, there are existing folktales and reenactments of performances which the directors and producers already know and they make efforts to reproduce those in films. Whenever the folktales are reproduced in video films, normally, by virtue of the previous awareness of the folktales by viewers, the film viewers are able to exhibit involvement in the film through participating in the forthcoming deed or mood. More often than not, viewers begin to act or laugh before the film actor, or even utter the lines as the actor articulate them on the screen of viewers' television, thus generating an instance of reproduction. Viewers' response to the line with or without the visual inducement discloses viewers' as having access to or likely to have exclusive understanding and close acquaintance with or knowledge of the film's plot. The reproduction revives such performances which are dying out, as these days there is a tremendous decline in traditional performances not only in northern Nigeria. Osofisan (2005:196) observes a similar trend in western Nigeria and labeled it "theatre crisis". According to him, "all the erstwhile theatre troupes have more or less disintegrated: all the actors dispersed into the video crowd in the manner that the popular Yoruba traveling theatre is no longer in existence". In the same manner, (Asaduddin and Ghosh 2012:xii) agree to this assertion as they express that, "video film as an art form has taken great strides and encroached upon realm and spaces formerly occupied by other art forms" Inevitably, this study asserts that some Kannywood video films and some actions embedded in some films such as *Daskin Da Ridi* and *Ruwan Bagaja* could be regarded as replica of earlier folktales in a new medium, even though Kannywood filmmakers engaged in copying Indian films at the early stage of the industry's inception. In essence, in the few Kannywood video films on cultural production of ancient folktales, conventional narratives and reenactments are replaced by their visual versions, thus shifting conventional narratives and reenactments into a more conclusive medium that take the place of more flowing oral versions. This development indicates that filmmakers became strongly attracted and interested by the visually striking display of moving images, which to a certain extent replaced a more synchronized correlation between two media. The relationship becomes more dynamic, composite and blended as the new medium integrate popular culture.

When there is contact between two cultures, local and foreign, more often than not the local culture is affected. In most cases, traditional ways of life are doomed to witness gradual or sudden change, the latter corresponding to a quick transition. Gradual change takes place slowly over a long period of time, sometimes spanning several generations. In the case of Hausa, the situation is an issue of cultural coalition. According to my observations, there is harmony between culture, media technology and globalization. Therefore, Kannywood filmmakers make use of this convergence and the video films are fused with existing cultural enactments.

The development symbolizes or exemplifies an emblematic endeavor to make perfectly clear what filmmakers hope could be recovered in imagination. Therefore, the reappraisal to traditional narrative composition, partly explains the rationality for film's on folktale success. For example, the Disney effect, procured traditional tales and remodeled them into mass-mediated films, notwithstanding the potentially inimical impact on the conveyance of the tales. In addition, the Cinderella story, a 2004 American film is a modernization of the classic Cinderella folktale and as Koven (2008:11) testifies, the film was told as a modern variant on the traditional fairy tale […] due to the easy equation between the evil mother in the film with the evil stepmother of the folktale.

Globalization, which is enhanced by the media has created the underlying support and starting point of the integration of invariable facts, details and both fictional and non-fiction stories on a large scale. Thus, the product of the homogenized information are transmitted to a widespread public organized into different groups including that which is recognized as folk or folktale imparting communities. Since the consequence of globalization is homogenization and mass-marketing of stories, filmmakers are bound to use stories from folktales and viewers are certain to consume and see some more identical cultural goods than discrete cultural products divided by national, cultural and linguistic frontiers.

In the contemporary period, as a result of the transition of folktales into films (e.g. Cinderella, Snow White and Tom Thumb children particularly, avail themselves of the film narratives and take advantage of such narratives to prearrange their own techniques of storytelling performance, to such an extent that film medium is obliterating traditional styles of stories. To this effect, Koven (2008:6) notes the importance of video-mediated narrative in developing the repertoires of the storytelling of children.

Video players were not available in the 1970s in mainly northern Nigeria, despite the general oil boom in the country. In the 1980s, the economy continued to depend heavily on imports due to the effects of the oil boom. As a result of mass importation, Nigeria witnessed the emergence of electronic media. Therefore, in the last three decades or so, a shift has taken place in Hausa culture. In place of the performance spaces, as Osofisan (2005:196) suggests, a new culture of information dissemination known as the video film emerged and has become the most popular and fastest growing means of cultural consumption in Nigeria today.

When there is contact between two cultures, local and foreign, more often than not the local culture is affected. In most cases, traditional ways of life are doomed to witness gradual or sudden change, the latter corresponding to a quick transition. Gradual change takes place slowly over a long period of time, sometimes spanning several generations. In the case of Hausa culture, the situation is an issue of cultural coalition. According to my observations, there is harmony between culture, media technology and globalization. Therefore, Kannywood filmmakers make use of this convergence and the video films are fused with existing set of story conventions such as narrations. Koven (ibid:6) labels these narrations media narraforms. He considers them as embodying a systematic relationship between the media and oral tradition. While the media provide the content, oral tradition provides the situations and format for the performance of these contemporary, hybrid narratives. By implication, there are recurring viewings of stories on video films, but also there is a high yielding inter-reliance between video, the contemporary device and orality, outmoded device. Although, the interdependence between the film device and the oral device has certainly manifested, however their continuous existence separately as individual entity is more or less doubtful, and as Koven (ibid:7) asserts, "the oral is more likely to die out so that the mass mediated could flourish and dominate".

Video film production requires directors to be more apt or appropriate in dealing with time compares to orality. While orality may spread out over a long time, a film must reduce to less than a performance would require a performer to perform a performance. Film has to be not only prompt, but also direct as a modern way of instantaneous communication. To a greater extent, film has to build up facts through several images that give information on story and character, all at the same time. By implication, while the director adds certain things, he has to cut some things which he considers less or not important from a video film's point of view. Thus, the process of elimination, which the director passes through accounts for the issue of fidelity in adaptation, the process of transforming or conversion of one genre such as folktale into another genre such as film. For the purpose of this study therefore, adaptation is a term for the process through which an old source is visualized on screen. More often that not, the old source serves as the starting activator for the film director which permits him or her to structure, form or interpret conceptually ideas of a certain cultural condition and human correlations embedded within its bounds.

Filmic Shifts on Folk Narrative Contents

A number of films trade in folktale medium. Hence, film is not only one considerable channel of imparting great deal of knowledge, but it is also a way of reflection of folktales. Besides, the conflict in folktale allows children to learn the tragic dimension of life, the battle between good and evil, between weak and strong and all that is good in the human spirit. Koven (2008:14) cites the *Kwaidon* (1964), a Japanese film as a cinematic retelling of Japanese ghost stories. Evidently, there abound folkloric elements and representations in films as a result of the appearance of the traditional folktale motifs in films such as *Puss in Boots* (2011) and *The Company of Wolves* (1984). Characteristically, such films with elements of folktales are based on or partly showcase nightmares concerning specific or extensive ancient taboos.

The traditional oral tale-types such as *Tortoise and the Hare, Lion and the Mouse and The Man and the Serpent* have been exceptionally prominent for a distinct and distant period in history among different communities especially for the moral lessons the tales disseminate. Therefore, filmmakers make good use of the opportunities offered by these tales. The filmmakers blend the horror in these fairy tales with images due to technology. As the case may be, the product - the film, serves as the return of folktale to its grown-up listeners through appropriating the visual images of the modern horror video film. Hence, the film looks obvious, without any attempt to be hidden from its appropriation of narratives, techniques, situations and set pieces from great older folktales.

As Helfield (2007:13) asserts, film on television evoke traditional rural culture, specifically the visible and rural signs and practices of French Canadian folktales [...] the formal elements of folk ritual are used in the films to reflect and express the effects of modernity on daily lives. Beyond merely reference to or integration of the essential or characteristic components of folk rituals, films in their utilization of images, narrative structural forms and manner or style of narration, films operate like folktales. This development may arise in relation to filmmakers fears of the threat of danger of cultural assimilation. The threats, more often than not, trigger filmmakers' individual cultural philosophies and ideologies, which aim is to preserve cultural heritage in particular and countryside and rural way of life in general vis-a-vis attempt to revitalize interest in local stories and fairy-tale and the comparable interest on untimely oral genres.

Notwithstanding the zeal for modernization, filmmakers nevertheless integrate and subsume folk traditions and ways of doing them into their films. In addition to narrations, viewers witness the insertion of folk songs of popular folksingers as well as folk dances as forms of socialization among locals. Evidently, filmmakers look back to folk songs and dances for ingenuity, creativity and inventiveness as embodiment of inspiration. They go by this, first, through uniquely adapting previous folk music, and secondly, through transforming words by placing them in the context of modern music and musical equipment to tally with or correspond to the social reality of the present time. Therefore, filmmakers return to the original by using well known (familiar conventions of) folktales in their video films to advance and actively support the creation and development of new fictitious lifestyle.

The method or process of looking back and contextualization adopted by filmmakers enhances the accessibility of folktales and their comparable films more easily. Hence, the more they are placed in the context of a local and identifiable background, the more evident their depictions of local cultural realities are manifested. Looking into the context of a previous folk narration for a new video film may take the format of mentioning a noticeable place, such as *Kogin Bagaja* (river bagaja) in *Ruwan Bagaja* (1998) or the use of a recognized local song for example, the use of the song of 'Dan'anace in *Karen Bana* (2012). Equally significant is the portrayal of the presence of the storyteller in the form of film's director in the film's storylines. The self-insertion of the director in the storylines, establishes him or her as an eyewitness to the folktale or one of the andiences when the follktale was narrated by an old woman or *amarya* (bride) through off-screen voice-over or through shots of the narrator narrating directly to the camera in the recording studio, thus positioning the folk narrator as both part of the ordering and a fundamental transmiter of the message.

Conclusively, the narrative elements of folktales used in films come up with momentous and significant links to the cultural past, thereby manifesting films as means of juxtaposition of traditional and modern styles of life, suggesting looking back to where a people came from as well as viewing how far they have gone. Therefore, the films on folktales draw others' awareness to salient shifts in society as well as the potentiality of traditional culture to bring to mind the expansion of new means of cultural revelation and portrayal. By implication, this assertion suggests that regardless of a film's material value and elegance or its technical intricacy or complication, the images a filmmaker uses to tell his or her story are often closely similar to traditional folktales. As Peterson (2007:93) expounds, "there is scarcely a tale which does not have its precursors, derivatives or analogous versions. Inevitably, tales evolve into other tales and replicate, elaborate, invert, abridge, link and comment on their own structure in an endless play of transformation". Therefore, the upward trend of global folktale is thus facilitated and precipitated by the potentiality of the global-culture industries to expropriate local images, modify, spread and disseminate them far away increasingly broad avenues of dispersal. Moreover, it also relies on the ability of local culture industries to echo, reproduce and modify techniques of communication to be convenient for or acceptable to local viewers.

One good example of an outstanding global folktale is the group of jinn tales, *Alf Layla wa Layla* (One Thousand Nights and a Night). It is remarkable for its potentiality instantaneously to juxtapose various components of binary opposition and pairs of distinctive features such as the noticeable and the unnoticeable, the insignificant and the significant, the dull and the attractive, functional and ruined. The folktales in the group have powerful correlations with some European folktales. Later, in the course of time, the modifying media industry has, over the years, extended the folktales into a spacious and large-scale valuable collection of tales and varieties of tales, which were made understandable and then conveyed in every medium fashioned by man-made technique comprising print and electronic mechanisms such as books and motion pictures. As Peterson (2007:99) expounds, "media industries are systems that appropriate cultural forms, reproduce them in transformed ways according to particular modes of production, and return them to public circulation in forms of recontextualization and remediation". Therefore, Peterson's aforementioned salient view calls attention for adaptation as a topic of consideration in dealing with a subject matter of filming folktales and theatre.

Adaptation as Valuable Resource in Filming

The procedure of conversion into film is an occurring phenomenon. Anne-Marie Scholz points out the idea of remaking stories into video films. Scholz (2013:1) states that remaking, "calls attention to the importance of the cultural phenomenon of adaptation in the history of film and television". She expresses how literary works have claimed to be boundless and virtually efficacious resource for filmmakers worldwide, since the innovation of moving images. In like manner, Dudley Andrew foregrounds how adaptation has been a strategy of filmmaking for a long time. According to Andrew (2000:28), "the making of film out of an earlier text is virtually as old as the machinery of cinema itself". Similarly Russell H. Kaschula (2001:xxx) states how Idrissa Ouedraogo was able to transpose onto film the most accurate techniques of African oral storytelling because of his background in storytelling and writing, even though there is a difference between oral storytelling and folktale adaptation. Notwithstanding the difference, Kaschula (ibid) describes Ouedraogo's films as "derivations of the techniques of oral tradition". The process of adaptation therefore, is an act of transforming one particular story in a particular genre to a story in another genre has both historical and cultural significance. Inevitably, stories which were initially in oral forms were converted into book forms, and the book forms are continually being transformed into films. As Farahmeen Munia (2017:4) states, "due to the technological advancement, like the Internet and electronic devices, adaptation of literary and non-literary works into visual medium has become very popular". Evidently, the popular film industry the Hollywood, right from inception, understood that it could undoubtedly attain reputation and legitimacy among viewers through reproducing respectable art as well as adapting literature to another medium especially film. In tracing some cases of adaptation, James Naremore (2000:4) states that, "film scholars such as William Uricchio and Roberta E. Peterson have shown how as early as 1908, at the peak of the nickelodeon boom and partly in response to the Reform Movement in American politics, the Vitagraph film company in New York have intensified efforts to appeal to the middle-class by engaging one reel adaptations of Shakespeare and Dante". At virtually the same moment, Parisian financiers established the Societé de Film d' Art, which made quite profitable feature films based on the dramas of Rostand and Sordou, as well as silent versions of Dickens's *Oliver Twist* and Goethe's *The Sorrows of Young Werthez* (ibid). Similar versions of art cinema sprang up, for example, in Brazil, where the works of novelist Jose de Alencar were adapted into numerous short films. Based on the numerous cases of adapted works, Naremore (2000:4) shows that, "for a while it seemed as if everything written, sung or danced for photographed ballet and opera formed a large part of the film d' art corpus in Western Europe between 1900 and the Renaissance and Greek tragedy as well, found its way into one of these stage-bound and pretentious productions".

It was evident that films, theatre and book publishing industry were growing together intimately to suggest that different creative media are constantly interwoven or intertwined, and in most cases, one new medium is interspersed in an earlier medium, in the sense that, a small medium becomes part of a larger medium. Specifically, Naremore asserts how, in the heyday of the classic studio system, Hollywood was absorbing every kind of artistic talent and establishing itself as the very emblem of modernity. In this regard, Naremore goes on to argue that, "certain films do not debase their literary sources instead they metamorphose novels into another medium that has its own formal or narratological possibilities" (2000:6). Naremore's opinion gives films artistic respectability based on the reason of modernist aestheticism. However, the explanation by Naremore suggests that, "the development is the confirmation that the intellectual priority and formal superiority of novels, which provide films their sources and with a standard of value against which their success or failure is measured is ascertained.

Inevitably, work on adaptation deals with transformed materials, which seem to violate or pervert their sources. As the case may be, the point is that, every material which is transposed intact to films is a representation, and as Naremore (2000:9) asserts, "every representational film can be regarded as an adaptation, and it is estimated that more than half of all commercial films are derived from novels". This statement seems as an exaggeration, however, Naremore (2000:11) shows how, "*The New York Times*, had in 1985, reported that one in fifty novels published in the United States were optioned by Hollywood [....] published statistics indicate how 20 percent of the films produced in 1997 had books as their sources, while others were derived from plays, sequels, remakes, television shows, and magazines or newspaper articles". In the same vein, Dennis Cutchins shows how films, texts and music, which people enjoy watching, reading and listening are comprehensively based on previous materials. Therefore, various medium deal with all or nearly all elements and aspects of adaptation. According to Cutchins (2014:41), "half the shows on Broadway or the West end are adaptations. More than half the films produced by Hollywood are adaptations. At least half the shows on television are either adaptations, or are based on true story. The literature we read and the music to which we listen constantly adapts texts, as well as genre and style". Inevitably, adaptation, remarking and every other form of retelling are now rampantly used by most film industries, especially in this age of mechanical reproduction and electronic communication. Therefore, adaptation in general has become part of filmmakers' strategy, and its constant adoption enables adaptation to change from the periphery to the middle of modern media studies.

This book is on the adaptation of orality into Kannywood video films of northern Nigeria. In this case, video film adaptation also described as transmutation, transfers a source material (orality) onto moving images (video film) as receptor material. Thus, the instruments and mechanisms are recognizably contrasting in nature from video film based on something else of a similar type. This development is synonymous to what Dudley Andrew (2000:28) says about film adaptation thus, "the matching of the cinematic sign system to prior achievements in some other system". Of great importance to video film are light, camera and sound, while storyteller's imaginations, use of gestures and emotions are the requirements for orality. Evidently, the implements for video films are distinct for orality and writing especially before the source material is successfully transferred onto screen. However, for the adaptation to be adjudged successful, it is paramount to make some interrogations such as: Are the characters in the source material the same in the video film version. Is the chronology of events of the story maintained in the film? As expected, the adapter by implication, the director of the video film version has to take into cognizance cultural knowledge. By inference, he has to consider the type of culture contained in the source material as well as the cultural point of view of the receptor material. One thing to consider about adapted film is that, no matter the questions and how the film is viewed, as Andrew (2000:ibid) asserts, "the process or the success of the film, its being owes something to the source that was its inspiration and potentially its measure". This development implies that the fundamental issues examined in a previous work are often the basic units from which the larger venture of film adaption is built up. In this direction, Constantine Santos (2012:xvii), in her analysis of epic film (a form of adaptation) expresses that, "the epic period should not be seen as a willing denunciation and abandonment of the earlier works nor is there a total break and radical division of the two periods. The period should rather be seen as a progression to more complex and more challenging enterprises...".

More often than not, the process involves one of the two: occasionally, the filming has to be carried out more or less faithfully, or sometimes, it has to be radically changed. Evidently, the scope of the storyline in the adapted film is expanded, severally beyond what the storyline in the original was offering. No matter which process is involved, the product that is the adapted film, as Naremore (2000:14) shows, "it brings orality and the cinematic into juxtaposition, reminding its audience that every medium is already intersected with multiple other media, suggest that a film can weave together multiple prior texts". In this development, it has been argued by Naremore that, "we now live in a media saturated environment dense with cross-references and filled with borrowings from books, films, and every other form of representation". Thus, this development is a circle full of metamorphosis, as books can transform into film, and film can turn into book, what Naremore describes as "published screenplays" (2000:13-14).

The source material for adaptation in this book center on storytelling, street performance, spirit-cult performance and occasional performance. These are varieties of what constitutes Hausa traditional theatrical forms. According to Munia (2017:23), "a film adaptation requires interpretation of certain issues in the language of film". Therefore, the work analyzes how some issues such as the magical potentiality of storytelling, the dis-junction – lack of correspondence or consistency and antagonism of good and evil and how their translation processes are accomplished completely and transferred successfully or otherwise onto the screen.

The source of the film be it folktale bears a transcendent relation to any and all films that adapt it. In this case, there is a need to look at the relationship between the structures of the literary and the adapted film. Given the differences between the two media, the questions especially of what are the losses, if any, and what are the gains? Have the characteristics of the literary retained or maintained in the adapted film? As Dudley Andrew (2000:28-29) expresses, "the film being a new artistic sign will then feature this original sign (from the source) as either its signified or its referent [...] then every cinematic rendering will exist in relation to some prior whole lodged unquestioned in the personal or public system of experience". In a summary manner and comprehensively, to a great extent, each adapted film as a characteristic adapts a prior formation. Indeed, the very term adaptation implies the continuous survival of a prototype. In the words of Jennifer M. Jeffers (2006:9), the original must have a copy in order to be valued as original. Characteristically, it would be right to suggest that adaptation has inherent feature such as appropriation of a meaning from an original text.

Unity of plot is the most evident problematic characteristics, mainly as a result of great length, which adapted films are more often than not unable to achieve. Evidently, the length of an adapted film becomes a crucial factor, especially when more space and time are required to accommodate more elaborate action sequences along with special effects and spectacle in general. Therefore, excessive length in adapted film, more often than not requires interlude, which function is to break the narrative flow of a lengthy film, in some cases making it difficult to retain the film's plot unity (Santos 2012:xxiii). The systemic model of adapted films, however are ascertained to some extent by literary sources from which they were extracted, but for the most part by the resolutions, which the director and his screenwriters made during the films' structure. This suggests that different directors have their own different methods of adapting literary material and they do not feel reluctant to fashion the plots as maintained by their narrative potentialities.

Adaptation and the Question of Fidelity

The concept of fidelity becomes a compelling discourse when it comes to the subject matter of adaptation. Inclined by this assertion is Jeffers (2000:19), who expresses that, "the concern with the fidelity of the adapted film in letter and spirit to its literary source has unquestionably dominated the discourse on adaptation [...] references are constantly made to what is left out or changed, instead of what is there". The reason for that is a simple fact that, there exists a general notion among critics that some adaptations are certainly more desirable, satisfactory, or effective, while others are not faithful to their sources. In this regard, Robert Stam (2000:54) expresses the predicament of viewers, especially when they consider that an adaptation has been unfaithful to the original. The term unfaithful, therefore, gives expression to the disappointment viewers feel when a film adaptation fails to capture what they see as the fundamental narrative, thematic, and aesthetic features of its literary source.

More often than not, when readers read a book, and viewers watch a film, there is no problem if both readers and viewers love what they read and watched. On the contrary, adapted versions are usually not worthy of that love, and the feeling of infidelity and betrayal come to mind when readers or viewers fail to realize some of the things that are most appreciated in the source materials. It is therefore a big challenge for filmmakers to obtain adequate creative visual imagination to showcase cinematic balance between source material and adapted version, and at most, brings out the equivalent of the style of the source material in the adapted material for viewers to see and appreciate. This is to show that there is an explicit, foregrounded relation of a cinematic text to a well-constructed original text from which it derives and which in some sense it strives to reconstruct. To this effect, Andre Bazin (2000:20) posits that, "faithfulness to a form, literary or otherwise, is illusory, what matters is the equivalence in meaning of the forms".

I am dealing in this book with two different artistic forms, orature on the one hand, and film on the other hand. The question that might come to mind is: faithfulness to what, and are adapters supposed to be faithful to the plot in all details? Bazin seems to suggest answer to this question as he says, it is perhaps not metaphorically impossible to make a cinematic work inspired by a literary one, with sufficient faithfulness to the spirit of the original and with an aesthetic intelligence that permits us to consider the film the equal of the book (2000:20). However, the matter of fidelity is not supposed to make us view it as an absolute filmic method, and a fundamental or proposition, which serves as the foundation for filmmaking. Evidently, the idea about fidelity in films is exceedingly difficult on some grounds as Stam (2000:55) expresses that, "it is questionable whether strict fidelity is even possible [...] an adaptation is automatically different and original due to the change of medium. In the script, it is written, in a film it is images and sounds".

More often than not, when a character is portrayed as handsome in orature such as folktale, it makes or compels the audience to imagine the character's distinctive attributes in their minds. By contrast, in a film, the character must be compelled to perform an audition for practical demonstration of his suitability and skill. In place of a character restricted to the imagination of listeners in orature, the listeners will come face to face with a clearly identified, specified and particular actor or actress in a film version of the same orature. On the one hand, the character in a novel or orature is designed to a fairly significant extent literally and orally that emerged from words. Therefore, he or she goes through a kind of process of breaking into fragments within the film adaptation. However, the character in an adapted film, by virtue of technology is more or less a mystifying merger of things such as photograph, body movement, acting style, and voice, which help to elaborate and add detail to storylines in conjunction with lighting, mise-en-scene, and music. Film adaptations have the overt interaction along with explicit reciprocal action and relationship between characters, thus predicting the possibilities of the existence of a model, and the appropriation of meaning from a prior text. More so, in a film a single actor or actress can take up more than one role. For example, Fati Mohammed plays both Zubaida and Azumi in *Sangaya* (2000).) Therefore, the scenario implies that film adaptation is a complex interplay of various images dealing with representation in connection with an earlier unmodified origin in the public or personal system of experience such as societal facet and individual behavior. This development suggests that the process of filmmaking alone necessitates the need to consider the demand for fidelity as secondary because the steps taken in film are capable of effecting differences between the original and the adapted, as Stam (2000:56) explains, "the very process of filmmaking – the fact that the shots have to be composed, lit, and edited in a certain way – generates an automatic difference".

It is pertinent to mention that there is the assumption that a nucleus central to the production of a particular film exists, which is to be conveyed and furnished by an adaptation. Hence, there is a high expectation from the admirers of fidelity to see the reproduction and or consideration of the essentials, the basics, the fundamentals, and the substance in an adapted film from orature as the original. But in dealing with two media, different in form, each medium may have a specific uniqueness procured from its separate substances of the action of making known one's thoughts and feelings. In addition to the change in medium, other eventualities also make fidelity in adaptation almost practically not possible and a seemingly unworkable task. For example, on the one hand a film is a collaboration and mobilization of crew, cast and supportive staffs, on the other hand, a novel can be written by one individual, and a performance might be performed by a single performer. In scripts written words are read while in films sounds are heard, and images, often called motion pictures are seen. To this effect, Stam (2000:57-58) assesses the contingencies of fidelity in adaptation, and asks the questions thus, "authors are sometimes not even aware of their own deepest intentions. How, then, can filmmakers be faithful to them? And to what authorial instance is one to be faithful? To the biographical author? To the textual implied author? To the narrator? Or is the adapter-filmmaker to be true to the style of a work? To its narrative point of view? Or to its artistic devices?"

Adaptation as a Model of Transformation

Adaptation aims at close connection rather than exactness. In this sense, the concept of the degree to which the result of adaptation conforms to the correct value of the original material is secondary, as relevance rather than accuracy is primary. This development implies that, adaptation demands the existence of a specific predecessor text or orature. From what is being adapted, by and large, there are always points of view, and specifically, there are actions and utterances, which are more often than not, influenced thus leading to similarities and difference in particular and transformation in general. This situation necessitates multiple readings, which is as a result of what Cutchins (2014:44) expounds thus, "the relationships, the simultaneous similarities and differences, between an adaptation and its source texts tend to generate readings, the hallmark of literary thought, and the central figure of the notion of adaptation".

In adapting orature to film, the director plays the role of not only an interpreter of the orature, but also a translator of it. Therefore, as the director serves these functions, he or she has to frequently negotiate the meaning of the orature in the new medium. In like manner, Jeffers (2006:16) expresses that, "the central issue in adaptation concerns transforming one medium into another". The director should be cognizant of a new context, which his or her viewers might generate. As the case may be, there is the possibility that viewers too are likely to interpret and translate the orature as they knew it before and as they watch a transformed version of it in a new medium. This situation of both director and viewer playing the roles of both interpreter and translator suggests the existence of implication for adaptation, as Cutchines (2014:46) expresses that, "texts are absolutely overflowing with meaning, and interpretation and retelling or adaptation of a text […] is liable to reveal or create even more new intended and unintended meanings".

It is worth mentioning here that a film adapter is not just telling a folktale or orature again or differently for viewers, but he or she is also, and at the same time reproducing the main ideas and words of the folktale. However, the adapter is not only unable to transport every meaning, but also he or she will have to inscribe numerous additional meanings, which he or she did not inevitably have prior intention as a direct consequence. This mention of numerous additional meanings, no doubt, confirms not only transformed folktale, but also new reading of it. Therefore, the actuality revisited in the film, the director of the film, the narrator of the folktale if at all he or she subsists, and the viewers, who re-enact and consequently, they are no doubt renewing the folktale, and at the same time, playing a part in the constituted world of the folktale.

Inclined by the assertion that adapted film participates in the represented world of folktale, I will affirm that the process of adaptation is radically a transformative process through which discrete people can learn to accept independent societies in particular and the world around them in general. Usually, filmmakers put to use newly arising prominent expressions and styles in local language. At the same time, filmmakers integrate sequence of borrowed words from foreign languages. Therefore, in adapted film in this form, viewers are engaged in interrogating the differences between original medium and adapted medium, by implication differences between local and foreign cultures. Subsequently, as Laurence Raw and Tony Gurr (2014:162) observed, "viewers tend to change their own view of the world by exposing their own cultural identity to the contrasting influences that the foreign culture and language might exert".

This situation suggests that, as processes of transfer and representation, adaptation is therefore, characterized as limitless, for the reason that within the confines of adaptation, there is not only the presence of globalizing world, but there is also the existence of the demanding willingness to change or compromise and due regard for differences in cultural traditions. Therefore, a film as a photographic image and sound enhances the ambiguous nature of adaptation, and at the same time elucidates on the different facets of adaptation. This development suggests that a source material, be it orature or text, after its adaptation generates a number of divergent critical readings. For example, *The Bridge on the River Kwai* (1957)[4], is one film, which received the

4   *The Bridge on the River Kwai* (1957) is an adapted film based on Pierre Boulie's novel, *Le Pont de la Rivière Kwai* (1952). The film's producer and director were American Sam Spiegel and British David Lean respectively. The film is an epic war film, which tells a historically based story of the construction of a railway in 1942-1943 from Singapor to Bangkok. While the novel upon which the film based its plot was considered as the bestselling novel, the film too, was included on the American Film Institute's list of best American film ever made besides many

most controversial discussion and critical readings of its time, thus the question about the film centers on, "is the film for or against war" (Scholz 2013:59). Based on that, attempts were made to define both what the film was and what it was not, precisely on the dual issues of anti-war and pro-war. Therefore, on the one hand, Scholz (2013:62) proposes that, "those who emphasized the anti-war aspects of the film paid less attention to specifically British themes and instead focused on its transnational character as, for example, a U.S. / British co-production based on a French text". On the other hand, those who hold up the claim of pro-war were of the opinion that indeed, a great proportion of war films were produced from U. S. and in that exact sense of the word, the producers had the fundamental and philosophical tendency to promote war due to the U. S. successes in previous wars. In addition, *Bridge* could actually imply an homage to British imperialism, to remind them of their previous colonial impact. More importantly, one film can be adapted severally with various transformations. Such transformation, which is as a result of adaptation, is what Jeffers termed as cultural cross – border raid, which occurs in film industry (2006:13). For example, the Hollywood film, *Bodyguard* (1992)[5] was adapted with the same title, *Bodyguard* by Bollywood film industry in 2011. Kannywood film industry followed suit and adapted *Bodyguard* in 2012 and gave it the title *Dogari* (Bodyguard), and subsequently, the Hong Kong Chinese film industry adapted *Bodyguard* in 2016. There is the tendency that the culture which is manifested in the original material is homogenized, even though adapted film is normally modeled on the local public's viewing tastes, irrespective of the original source material. Thus, the homogenization process leads to assemble of local specificity, which surrounds local identity. Evidently, *Dogari* (2012) (Bodyguard), fits the narrative structure of Kannywood films, with emphasis on long dialogues, humour and exaggeration to suit local audience. Therefore, the director as an adapter chooses to remake *Bodyguard* according to his target viewers' local conventions. As Raw and Gurr (2014:166) stated, "an adapter has

awards given to it.

5   *Bodyguard* (1992) is a film about a famous music star, Whitney Houston. When Houston starts receiving death threats from an unknown stalker, she is compelled to hire Kevin Costner to protect her. Costner, a former secret service agent became a bodyguard. Therefore, Houston hires him as a bodyguard to guard her at all costs because of the stalker's terrorist threats. Eventually, Housten and her bodyguard, Costner start a romantic affair.

the freedom to manipulate the source material so as to accommodate the demands of the target audience – for example local readers or film-goers".

The impression set up by Raw and Gurr is that adapters have certain privilege and potentiality to put up their own materials with little perturb for fidelity. However, Stam (2000:63) shows how Sergio Giral's adaptation of Cuba's first antislavery novel was not only "sarcastically faithful" to the sentimental spirit of the novel, but it was also a "realistic reconstruction" of the historical life of the enslaved. In a related manner, Roger Manvell (1979:93) cites how, *Three Sisters*, a play by Anton Chekhov, written in 1901 passed through adaptation into three different film versions, first, in 1964 for Mosfilm, directed by Samson Samsonov, and secondly, in 1966 by the American Actors Studio, and thirdly, the British version was filmed by the National Theatre in 1970.

The artistic and technical mediation between source material in this work and the new medium – film is likely to demonstrate exaggeration of the source material through its filmic equivalent, thereby causing and generating cinematic transformation. Besides, other technicalities that might intensify filmic transformation include the adapter's ability to focus on what the source material insinuates, rather than sticking fast to the exact thing a character says or does in the source material. Secondly, the adapter should aspire to look beyond the surface level of the source material and then identify what he or she believes is the meaning, message or theme of the source material. By doing so, viewers might have a feeling of creative and productive transformation of the source material the adapter uses and imbibes in their minds. For example, Scholz shows how Sam Spiegel related *The Bridge on the River Kwai* (1957), an epic war film as a love story between a man and his bridge, a tragic anti – war picture that differed from the predominantly satirical tone of Pierre Boulle's novel from which the film was adapted (2013:55). In this manner, more often than not, adapted films or works generally generate multiple readings, thereby giving consideration to explicit individual points of view. Invariably, different perspectives are likely to manifest, which are aimed towards juxtaposition, especially between the source material and the adapted film, thus establishing the likelihood and feasibility of vigorous portrayals or public reactions as a result of transformation and several facets in the adapted film. As one would expect, the composite and ambiguous nature of renditions of adapted films would invoke the relationship between the orality dominated past and filmic present. As Jeffers (2006:9) foregrounds, an invented tradition is also more triumphant when the rapid transformation of society weakens or destroys the social patterns for which old traditions had been designed, which undoubtedly describes our own digital age".

Roger Manvell comments on *Pygmalion*, a play by Bernard Shaw, which was adapted into film. Manvell (1997:62) recounts how Shaw expresses delight as he says, "my stuff is as good on the screen as on the stage". However, Manvell explains how adaptation gives room for expansion to some extent in order to allow the addition or insertion of visual action, thus making substantial adjustments. This development suggests the concept of transformation. As Manvell (ibid:62) foregrounds, the adapters of Shaw's work, altered it out of all recognition. They spoiled every effect, falsified all the characters, put everything Shaw left out in and took out most of what he had put in. They cut out half of his dialogue in order to insert dozens of changing pictures between the lines of what was left, seemed to the producers indispensable.

In a different dimension, Manvell's observation is contrary to the opinion proposed by Jeffers (2006:14), who argues that "the very subject of film adaptation poses the problem of copy to the original instead of original to copy". Evidently, the environment of the source material, in the case of this work, orality, is transformed due to the chain of events that precede a film adaptation, especially images from the film, and the quality and ability that may develop and lead to media publicity. This development insinuates the concept of adapted film's transformation in relation to flow due to the insertion of more recurrent commercial breaks, which are blended into the sequence. In addition, a voice-over may be used to serve as a necessary background fact, as in *Karen Bana* (2013), so that the action will be justifiable and practicable for the viewers. Fundamentally, the voice-over is an economically worthy and acceptable means for adaptation because some sentences of elucidation may be looked attentively at before considering it into a few minutes of oral narration. Thus, the adapted film remains, therefore, an engrossing and fascinating hybrid, situated to some extent across the space separating orality on arena and on screen.

The manoeuvre across events on the arena and on the screen, therefore, requires a filmmaker's consideration which, while it seems nothing out of the ordinary, but it is astonishing and impressive. Therefore, the filmmaker has to consider a number of things such as some words from the original source, the filmmaker's conceptualization of the original source, the accurate reading of the source material, and the constraints the filmmaker has, as a result of the inevitable transformative nature of adaptation, which Cutchins foregrounds that, "adaptation will never be able to convey all of adapter's meanings, but at the same time will offer many more meanings that an adapter did not necessarily intend" (20014:47). This development suggests that inventiveness and embellishment are basic realities attached to adapted films, nevertheless, Jonathan Rosenbaum (2000:209) shows that, "it is naive to assume that the best film adaptation can provide precise equivalents to each of the elements in the originals".

Some notable forms of change, which constitute and promote transformation in adaptation, at least from the point of view of Manvell include insertion, omission and substitution. Manvell provides an example from the adaptation of Electra, a play to film. Manvell expounds the most notable differences between the original play and the adaptation. According to him, the changes were made possible through the insertion of a brilliantly conceived mimed prelude at the beginning of the film […] and the omission altogether of the intervention by the gods at the end, and substituting the far more mundane hostility of the peasantry against the matricides...(1979:83). The idea here suggests that for transformation to function and become workable, it has to go through certain changes, focusing on particular actions, which conjointly, are instrumental to the changes in adapted medium vis-a-vis wider shifts in society.

More often than not, it is the conflation of two media: play and film for example, gives to viewers much of the adapted film's distinguishing and indispensible quality, thus manifesting the links between the original source, film and the subsequent transformation. Since direct adaptation to filmic action is more or less difficult, therefore, the strategy for the transformation, as Manvell discloses in addition to the above, has to be through cutting back rigorously the lengthier speeches and interchanges of dialogue suitable only for projection from a stage, and by reenacting in mime certain actions of the story, past and present, which are recounted in the play as part of its purely verbal exposition, thus bringing together for the film version the maximum possible continuity of action (1979:86)

One outstanding thing to consider within the prevalent domain of transformation in adaptation, is the ability of an adapter to attain an astonishing stability between the necessary condition of either a play or folktale as the original material, and the need or demand of a film as an adaptation. To achieve the balance, focus should be on movement and visual interest, which will provide access or an opportunity to perceive the intended meaning of the actions of the characters and interpret them in a particular way, giving suitable prominence to dialogue. In this case, therefore, the adapter or director of the adapted film should explore the potentialities of film in conformity to specifically conventional stylistic pattern to be shown on screen.

Conclusion

As it is portrayed in this chapter, adaptation is not on the edge of filming. Rather, it covers to an important degree, a thorough explanation or investigation of all artistic undertakings. This assertion proves itself as it is generally and broadly acknowledged that, for quite a long time, there has been a considerable shift of adaptation from text to text to adaptation from folktale to newer medium such as video film. By implication, filmmakers who adapt are by all means ditching the past and reinventing themselves in a new medium, thereby repackaging culture and selling it back to themselves in particular and to viewers in general. Invariably, the motivation on part of the filmmakers to adapt folktale to film is enhanced by the cultural acceptabilities and issues involved in the transformation. As adaptation entails sharing boarders between new medium and previous medium suggests that, the very act of adaptation, inevitably creates even more meanings or the necessity of multiple readings for which those seeking to acquaint with the new medium must account.

Filming folktales is thus involved in the circle of adaptation of orality, creating it in the boundless and unlimited process of renewal and transformation. Therefore, film is viewed as a kind of multi-layered negotiation of media. On the one hand, the process is often productive as it calls for folktales to be retrieved, recovered and make more exciting, interesting and tantalizing by film. On the other hand, it affords film the means to illuminate folktale as a source material for filmmaking. In the process, the imagery of apparition hinted at directly in the folktale, *Ruwan Bagaja* for example, does not only make its way on to the screen, but it is also seen in full for the first time on screen. This is in particular an astonishing and remarkable dimension of adaptation. It takes a story the audience are told, and show it to them on the screen, leaving no time for imagination. Rather, the scenario creates viewers' and reviewers' comments about the degree of fidelity and originality the adaptation manifest clearly towards its presumed source material. This development suggests that many viewers form an opinion or conclusion about film adaptations by contrasting and noting the similarities or dissimilarities between them and the original source. However, the important values that form vital role in appraisal of adaptations that lean on a film's fidelity to its source material have been, to a great extent demeaned by scholars. These scholars move beyond the fidelity approach by foregrounding a variety of issues relevant and suitable to a constructive judgement of adaptations. Thurs, they point to the ingrained differences of the two media of folktale and film, the qualities of being specific in the production process, technological innovations, and to cultural contexts at the time of both the source material and the adaptation, are of course some vital issues that should be considered.

4 HAUSA PERFORMING ARTS IN CONTEMPORARY SOCIAL LIFE

In this chapter I explore the historical background of the Hausa with emphasis on their identity and where they are found. The chapter also discusses some types of Hausa conventional performances: firstly, performances for achieving religious purposes, such as *bori* and *tashe*; secondly, performance for the aristocrats, such as *wasan gauta* and court singers. By doing so, the chapter made it possible to understand how people relate to Kannywood video films in addition to emphasizing and drawing attention to the affiliation between Hausa orality and its transition. This suggests that people could be able to get a slightly better understanding of the transformation of not only Hausa oral performances, but also culture in general if they could carefully relate the correlation of paternity between Hausa conventional performances and Kannywood video films. This aspect of connection can be achieved through the exploration of the conventional forms of performing arts. Besides, people's understanding can be influenced through analysis of some selected video films, which is undertaken in chapter six.

Historical Background of the Hausa People

Before investigating metamorphosis of oral performance in Kannywood video films, a quick look at the historical background of the Hausa people, the types of performances they practice and the current status of the performances is essential. The term Hausa refers to native speakers of the language as well as to neighbouring ethnic groups, who have adopted it as their first language. Specifically, Newman (2000:1) states that it is the language of ethnic Hausa and settled Fulani in what one might call Hausa land proper. Similarly, Jaggar (2001:1) claims that as a result of historical contact, mother-tongue speakers of Hausa include many ethnic Fulani.

The Hausa people form one of the three largest ethnic groups in Nigeria often referred to as the "Big Three", i.e. Hausa, Ibo, Yoruba (arrangement based on alphabetical order). Kano, Nigeria, for quite long a centre of commerce, contains the largest concentration of the speakers of Hausa. Indeed, Kano can be said to be the modern capital of Hausa speakers. Also, the Hausa can be said to form the biggest group in the

Niger Republic. There are said to be more than a million Hausa speakers in the Republic of Sudan (Ahmed, 2000:32). According to Argungu (in Abu-Manga, 1999:7), the Hausa community in the Sudan is believed to be the largest Hausa Diaspora in the world. The permanent settlement of the Hausa communities in the Sudan could be understood as the result of what Abu-Manga describes as pilgrimage to Saudi Arabia with hardship (ibid). While some travellers completed the journey after many strenuous years, others became stranded on the way and ended up settling themselves permanently in other countries. R. C. Abraham (1946) reports an example of such instance, as quoted in Abu-Manga (1999: 8),

> …while en route to Eritrea via the Sudan, I was amazed to see a young girl selling bean-cake and calling out waina! Waina! She told me that she was of Kano origin and that there were many hundreds of Hausas living in Wadi Medani like herself. These people of Wadi Medani and many towns of Sudan were Hausa pilgrims to Mecca who ran short of money on their return and were unable to make their way back to their home towns in Nigeria. They have retained Hausa and taught it to their children born in Sudan.

There are also communities of Hausa in Ghana, Togo, Benin, Cameroon and Chad. According to Ahmed (2000:32), the Hausa settlers have been established in these areas since a fairly long time, certainly before the coming of the Europeans to West Africa. The Hausa distinguish between seven proper Hausa states called *Hausa bakwai*, the seven Hausa states, and *Banza bakwai*, the seven illegitimate Hausa, the latter being ethnic groups who have been under Hausa influence for a long time and have therefore partly or wholly adopted the language and civilization of the Hausa. The *Hausa bakwai* are the cities: Biram, Katsina, Zazzau (Zaria), Kano, Rano, Gobir, Daura. The *Banza bakwai* are: Zamfara, Nupe, Kebbi, Gwari, Yauri, Ilorin (Yoruba), Kwararrafa (Jukun). Bargery (1934:XI) cites Ibn Batuta's testimony regarding these Hausa states, as he claims that "it is evident that about the middle of the fourteenth century at least some and probably all of the Hausa lived in the country which they inhabit today, and it is likely that they had already been living there for centuries". In Nachtigal's opinion, according to Bargery, the Hausa came from the east, whereas Barth is convinced that they are a branch of the

Berbers (Amazigh) in North Africa, who immigrated into their present residences about A.D. 1000 (XI).

Another assertion related to the Hausa, which of course is the most often attested tradition, is the legend of Bayajidda. According to this legend, a certain Arab adventurer called Bayajidda came to Daura in present Katsina state, Nigeria around the first century A.D. and killed the mighty snake of the "Kusugu" well. His act of bravery enabled him to marry Damagaram, the Queen of the town. She gave birth to a son called Bawo, and Bawo in turn begot six sons, who along with Biram (Bayajidda's son born at Gaya before he arrived Daura when he left Borno) founded the seven Hausa states above. Summarily, the term Hausa is the name of a language and of a people, however, what remains a fact is that today Hausa remains a jumbled mishmash of ethnic groups. In this regard, Bargery (1934:XII) claims that it would appear true to assume the existence of a basic group of people associated with Hausa.

However, the original group of people that formed the nucleus of the Hausa of today had in their early history been expanded and in fact transformed by immigration from the north and east. Cultural events in Hausa society are enclosed with forms of performances such as singing, dancing, drumming, and rituals. This justifies the assertion that performances are forms of religious and social acts among all the world's cultural communities, including Hausa. From the point of view of the past religious and present cultural experiences within Hausa social structure, this chapter considers two main categories of Hausa performance. These are oral performances for religious purposes and oral performances for entertainment.

Oral Performances for Religious Purposes

Religion is considered as the earliest source in the manifestation of performance in particular and drama in general, as Roscoe (1971:176) claims, "it is hard to find scholars who would challenge the view, that drama's roots lie in religious and quasi – religious practices". Like other communities, the Hausa have had an earlier religion. Evidently, before the Hausa had contact with the Berbers, the Asbenawa (Tuaregs), the Mandingoes and the Europeans, they practised a traditional religion. The worship of spirits known as "iskoki" constituted their religion. At Dala rock in Kano lived Barbushe, the priest of a spirit called Tsumburbura who dwelt in a sacred tree and received sacrifices of goats and fowls from his worshippers. Jigawa and neighbouring villages around Gwarzo were inhabited by Hausa in the pre-Islamic age. During traditional ceremonies, the priest, Barbushe, exercised a ritual jurisdiction and leadership in concert with other senior lineage heads. This religion, according to Kofoworola and Lateef (1987), is one of the earliest standing points of Hausa performing arts. It is based on the existence of some invisible or spirits called *iskoki*. The Hausa believe that the spirits have powers which are capable of controlling people's lives, their fortune and even their daily affairs and issues of their state of being or existence. Based on the acceptance of the existence of the spirits and on curiosity, the Hausa then try to unfold the obscure matters of the natural world around them by making efforts to understand the power of nature with the sole aim of making it to work in their favor. To accomplish this, a religious form of performance, which serves as a means of communication to the invisible spirits with the intention that they could draw the attention of the spirits to the solution of their problems, is employed. Such problems could be various forms of life's experiences: disease, drought, and war. It is not an overstatement therefore when Bauman (1977:32) shows how performance can involve healing by using specific curing chants. The idea of invoking the unseen forces developed into what can be described as *bori* among the Hausa.

Bori as Ritual

The earliest religious practice in the ancient Hausa speaking areas before the advent of Islam in Hausa land is *bori*. It is similar to voodoo, a form of magic practised in the Caribbean, especially Haiti. However, voodoo is said to have its origin from West Africa. Nowadays in Hausa society such belief and practice are looked upon contemptuously and it is considered not only as superstitious belief and practice, but as *kafirci* (not believing in God) as well, at least among Muslims. In support of this fact, Ahmed (2000:41) says that *bori*'s polytheistic and pantheistic features are contrary to Islam, and there is little wonder therefore that *bori* has disappeared considerably in Muslim Hausa community, although there are still some traces of adherents of *bori* among Maguzawa[6]. Our concern is this study is not to debate on the status of *bori* now, but to discuss it as an earlier form of Hausa performance and how it serves as a means of entertainment that involves some kinds of demonstrations to enhance the audience's appreciation and pleasure during events such as wedding and naming. However, when not undertaking these normal life ceremonies, it is believed that *bori* performance must take place in special locations such as under the baobab, tamarind trees and riverside areas in order to ensure their effective response or intervention. These locations are believed to be the dwelling place of the spirits in addition to *Birnin Jangare*[7]. There is no certainty regarding where the city of *Jangare* is situated as there are only conflicting pieces of evidence. While some believe that *Jangare* is by the east of Hausa land, others say it is around Argungu in Kebbi State, whereas some people are of the opinion that it is in the south of Kano (Umar, 1982). As a ritual, *bori* consists of two major groups, the "invisible" and the "visible", and each group has class or hierarchy based on the importance of the spirits and the adherents of *bori* in the cult. While the invisible group consists of *Ubangiji* (Lord) as the supreme leader and then the *Iskoki* (spirits), the visible group consists of *Boka* (traditional healer, native doctor, wizard) and `*Yan bori* (Bori cultists) and then other people who consult *boka* or `*yan bori* for fortune telling and medicine.

Bori as Performance

As a performance, *bori* is normally an annual event although it is performed occasionally whenever a need arises. No matter when it is performed, before the performance, adequate arrangements have to be done. These include fixing a day for the performance, sending invitations to musicians, other fellow *bori* cultists from far and near and other personalities who may not necessarily be *bori* cultists, but are affiliated to it in one way or another. Various reasons necessitate *bori* performance. For example, *bori* is performed for curative purposes i.e. to cast out a

---

6   *Maguzawa* pl. Bamaguje sg. Mas. *Bamagujiya* sg. Fem. These are Hausa who do not practice neither Christianity nor Islam as a religion. Based on this, they are regarded as pagan Hausa. More often than not, they live in rural areas where they can practice *bori* without much persecution.

7   It is believed among adherents of *bori* that apart from the sacred abodes of the spirits, there is a big city mainly of the spirits called *Birnin Jangare* (the city of Jangare*)*

spirit which is tormenting someone. Kofoworola and Lateef (1987:7) explain that:

> It is assumed that the *bori* performance involves such serious objectives as searching for the solutions to curative crisis, psychological and social conflicts, confrontations and other forms of disorderliness.

It is also performed for the purposes of wedding, naming and coronation. In his observations, Andrew Horn (in Kofoworola and Lateef, 1987) outlines that:

> There are four distinct types of *bori* performance, two of which are primarily for public amusement and two of which are intended to achieve communication with the *iskoki,* spirits (1987:7).

Bori performance like other performances is characterized by the use of costumes. During *bori*, each *ɗan bori* (bori cultist) wears special costume that relates to the spirit he possesses and then goes to the venue which is usually a field and joins with the others. While `yan bori* converge on one side of the field, the musicians take the other side and the spectators rally round the field. The performance begins with a welcoming speech by a *boka* (traditional healer) or a renowned *ɗan bori*. After the speech, the musicians start drumming and singing praises or epithets of the spirits. Each *ɗan bori* that hears the epithets of the spirit which possessed him becomes irritated and then starts jumping and falling on the ground with his buttocks. He claims being possessed by a spirit therefore he begins to mimic the spirit by which he is known to have been possessed. For example, he who is possessed by the spirit *Malam Alhaji* (Mr. Alhaji), behaves like an Arab and talks using words like Arabic. He who is possessed by the spirit *Bebe* (dumb man) imitates a dumb person. Similarly, he who is possessed by the spirit *Kuturu* (leper) makes fists by curling his fingers tightly towards the palm of his hand. When it is realised that the *ɗan bori* is fully possessed, *boka* then sings the epithet of the spirit tormenting the *ɗan bori*, as well as murmuring in the form of incantation to indicate that he is receiving instructions from the spirits. Thereafter, he is heard giving thanks along with epithets. This shows that success is achieved. At times the *boka* is heard apologizing and begging, indicating that the spirit is annoyed. This process goes on until a possessed *dan bori* is dispossessed and has fully come back to his senses, then musicians stop drumming and spectators go back home.

Bori Initiation Rites

Bori has a special initiation rite known as *girka*. When someone is sick, usually *boka* makes attempt to cure him. But when the sickness persists, he advises that the assistance of `yan bori has to be sought in order to set the sick person free from the spirit that possesses him and ensures the sickness. Sometimes, it is said, if you cannot defeat them, join them. Based on this assertion, the *boka* postulates that there has to be a means of persuading the spirit to remain with the sick person in form of his mentor. The *boka* has the prowess to know which spirit has possessed the sick person therefore he takes the responsibility of training him how to live peacefully with the spirit. Some of the materials for the initiation are: mats, wrappers, one white and black chicken, concoction, perfume and decorated calabash.

While the person undergoing initiation sits on a new mat and covers his or her head with a white wrapper, the two chickens are slaughtered. The *boka* performing the initiation keeps the white chicken on the head of the person undergoing initiation while he puts the black chicken on his shoulder and then goes round the sick person three times. After this episode, he consults the spirits. He persuades some of the spirits and then asks if they will settle down with the sick person. The persuasion and the questions continue until demand is achieved. The sick person is asked to walk backwards, jumps and falls on the ground with his or her buttock and instructed not to talk to anyone for three days. During this period, his or her food and drink are mixed with concoction. On the third day, which is called *fasa baki* (break the silence), the sick person cleans his or her mouth and eyes with a cotton sucked in concoction and after answering a call from *boka,* he or she can resume talking. On the last day of the initiation, there are varieties of food and live chickens. *Boka* prays, slaughters the chickens and then takes off the white wrapper covering the head of the sick person. He or she then bathes with concoction, after which he or she is asked to dress up properly. From then, the person is initiated and becomes *dan bori* and whenever he or she hears the epithets of the spirit which possesses him or her, he or she becomes possessed immediately. Usually, *bori* initiation rite ceremony takes three to seven days. However, depending on the sickness which may necessitate *girka* (initiation), it can last for two or three weeks and even three months.

It is pertinent to mention that *bori* is discussed here in the context of performance due to its form. It is an enactment that comprises qualities such as "unauthentic" and "imitation". For example, the enactment of speaking Arabic by a *bori* cultist who is possessed by Mr Alhaji is unreal. Second, the costume he wears and the words he utters are only to simulate an Arab. He changes his real or genuine behaviors through imitation. He transforms through his attire, speech and the manner he behaves. In general, the appearances of *bori* cultists during *bori* are out of the ordinary when they are compared to their everyday or normal modes of actions. Therefore, *bori* is considered as a performance based on its mimetic characteristics.

Tashe Performance

The word *tashe* is a derivative of the word *tashi* which means to wake up, to get up and to fly. All these three senses of *tashi* are significant and relevant in the context of *tashe.* While to wake up and to get up are relevant in the sense of getting up from sleep in the early hours of the morning when the light is beginning to appear; in order to start fasting, to fly deals with a type of *tashe* known as *zan tashi* (I will fly). What makes *tashe* a performance for religious purposes is firstly its popularity among Muslims in Hausa community. Secondly, it is performed during the month of Ramadan i.e. when Muslims are expected to fast for one month. The performance begins after fasting for ten days and continues up to the eve of the Idel-Fetri celebration. The purpose of the *tashe* performances are: First, to awake the Muslim populace to prepare for the next fasting day; second, to lure Muslims away from non-Islamic leisure or pastimes since the fasting month of Ramadan is a holy month to Muslims; third, to entertain, since the performers and the audience feel happy, especially that the audience would like to relax and enjoy their time, particularly after completing the fast for that day (Ahmed, 1985:37). *Tashe* is more common among the youths. However, adults also take delight in performing it and some *tashe* are exclusively performed by them only. The performers usually move from house to house and after each performance, the audience give the performers gifts in cash or in kind. Some examples of *tashe* performances are: *Ka Yi Rawa Kai Malam* (You Have Danced You Teacher), *Jatau Mai Magani* (Jatau the Healer),

Kamun Gwauro, (The Divorcee Arrest), *Haƙuri Yaya,* (Be Patient Elder Sister), *Mairama da Daudu* (Mairama and Daudu).

Ka Yi Rawa Kai Malam

Ka yi rawa kai Malam requires someone to act as *Malam* and some three or four other performers. The concept of *Malam* in this description corresponds to the assertions of Umar (1980:19) and Ahmed (1985:39). The scholars claim that the status of *Malam* in the performance is similar to what is obtainable in normal life situations where he is considered as someone who is learned in the Qur'an, someone worthy of a pious man and an instructor. Therefore, to meet some of the characteristics of the learned ones, the *Malam* in the performance improvises beard and moustache with cotton in order to make him resemble the learned clerics. He then holds a rosary, a jug for ink, a skin of ram for prayer and a slate. The performance is carried on along with a song; the *Malam* serves as the chorister while other performers serve as the lead vocalists. In the song, the vocalists make a mockery of the *Malam* by affirming that he has turned away from the path of righteousness by dancing. As a cleric, he is supposed to be gentle and decent, but not engaging in dancing which is considered as *bidi'a* (drumming, singing and dancing) among some sects, an attribute not worthy of a religious leader. In his response, he denies the allegation. First, he says, "No, I did not dance." Second, he shows to the vocalists, the rosary, the jug, the skin of ram and the slate which indicates that he still worships Allah and remains a Muslim cleric. However, despite the denial of having danced, he later dances a little because he finds the song soft, melodious and soothing.

Kamun Gwauro

Kamun Gwauro (the divorcee's arrest) is a popular *tashe* performance. It is performed by male adults and the idea behind the performance is to signify the importance of getting married. The person who takes the lead role, the *gwauro* (male divorcee) wears a gown, holds a torch light and then rides a donkey. Other performers serve as musicians and follow him, playing music with tins and broken calabashes and together they walk towards the residence of a male divorcee. As soon as they find a victim, they dress him in a gown made of tattered mat and put on his neck a necklace of groundnut dumplings. The performers then instruct the divorcee to simulate the cry of various animals. The significance of the performance is to provoke the divorcee. The performers have the opinion that if they provoke the divorcee, he will be motivated to marry before the next fasting period.

Jatau Mai Magani

This performance requires that the lead actor who is a *jatau* (healer) gets various herbs in a basket or bag or sack. It does not really matter if he uses special costumes, although he is supposed to appear like a *boka* (traditional healer) with charms on the waist and armlets on the arms and then to hold a short axe. *Jatau* then takes each herb, mentions its name, explains how it is used and then takes it back to the container. The performance is done along with a song led by Jatau and the rest of the performers answer in chorus.

Haƙuri Yàayaa

This performance does not require special costumes. However, it requires household materials or kitchen utensils like dishes, plates, frying pan, pots, spoons, and knives which the performers carry along with them. In most cases, used or out of use household items are employed as new materials are not necessarily required. When the performers arrive at the scene of the performance, they throw the materials on the floor or ground and then the *Yàayaa* (Elder sister), who plays the role of the leader of the performance as well as lead vocalist begins to pick the materials one by one. As she picks them, she keeps saying that she is going back home (to her parents). She means that she is tired of her marriage because her husband curses and scuffles her all the time. While she complains, other performers keep on begging her to be patient and remain in her matrimonial home. The performance is performed along with a song led by *Yàayaa* and the rest of the girls chant "*haƙuri Yaya*" in chorus.

Mairama da Daudu

This performance has three parts and it is usually performed by girls. Part one is the prelude, the preparation for the main event and arrival to the venue. While part two is the main performance, part three is the farewell and the subsequent movement to the next venue. Each part is performed along with a special song. The lead performers are called Mairama and Daudu, from whom the name of the performance is derived. They take the roles of bride and bridegroom respectively even though the bridegroom is played by a girl. On arrival to the venue of the performance, Mairama and Daudu hide behind a door or tree while other performers set Mairama and Daudu's seats and place items such as mats, jugs, dishes and plates to commemorate a household along with the materials that are commonly seen at home. As the arrangement is going on, one of the performers is singing and others answer in chorus.

When the residents of the compound succumb to the call by coming out to see the performance, the performers then usher Daudu to his seat before ushering Mairama. When each of them takes a seat, their heads are unveiled and the performers sing their praises, starting with Daudu. They associate Daudu with good leadership qualities by pointing out hard work and courage as his attributes and then urge women to marry him because by virtue of his bravery, he can surely protect not only the womanly of the womenfolk, but he can as well ensure their security. As for Mairama, the performers assign to her the attributes of a virtuous woman. They present her as a courageous, polite, submissive woman who will not show co-wife rivalry. In this part, all the performers act as lead vocalists, therefore the songs have no chorus.

Like other oral genres, Hausa oral performances are handed over from one generation to another through narration, memoralization and eventually training only. This is due to the absence of any system of writing in the early Hausa society hence during that preliterate period the only type of literature must remain oral, often referred to as *adabin baka*[8]. Oral literature including performances continues to be the source or medium of entertainment until the beginning of the massive production of electronics. Hausa oral performances are numerous and, as Skinner says, the Hausa have a tradition of arts. There exist performances of tales, praise songs and poetry, sometimes involving gesture or music[9]. For the

---

8 Hausa literature is classified into two major parts of written literature and oral literature. While written literature comprises prose, peotry and drama, oral literature which is called *adabin baka* in Hausa comprises folktales, songs, performances, proverbs, tongue twisters etc. For a full classification of Hausa literature, see Ɗangambo Abdulƙadir *Rabe-raben Adabin Hausa Da Muhimmancinsa Ga Rayuwar Bahaushe* (1984)

9 Hausa oral arts involving performance include *tatsuniya* (tales), *labaru* (traditions), *kirari* (epithets), *wasanni* (plays), *karin magana* (proverb), *waƙoƙi* (songs), *kacici-kacici* (riddles), and *salon magana* (tongue twisters). See, Skinner Neil (1980)

purpose of this study, oral performance for the aristocrats and oral performance for the commoners shall be considered.

Oral Performance for the Aristocrats

Politically, the early Hausa society was organised based on kinship: families and clans. When the population started to increase and urbanization came up, power to control people was shared between the custodians of ancestral cults and the traditional rulers. The highest rank a leader can attain is *Sarki* (chief). Although *Sarki* is considered as the chief executive, he has some council officials with whom the affairs of the town are managed in the palace of the chief. In such a setting, performances are carried out as elaborate and organised form of entertainment.

Wasan Gauta

Wasan gauta is performed at the palace by mainly the concubines who usually get the full support and view of the chief, his courtiers and officials of the royal administration. It is a comical and satirical performance which is performed only once in a year. The participants assign to themselves the personalities of certain officials including the chief himself and they try to imitate their characters in front of the audience and send them certain messages about their chief, his courtiers and officials of the royal administration. The actresses employ various forms of imitations and gestures to simulate their masters in addition to wearing men's cloth. They strive hard to imitate and reproduce all manners of characters and behaviours so that the audience would recognize the person being imitated. Although, the objective of this performance is to entertain, but from a critical point of view, it functions as a check and balance in the administration of the palace. It does not only draw the attention of the chief to issues of the palace, making him aware of certain behaviours of some of his council officials, but it makes him aware of some of his personal weaknesses, too, so that he could rectify the situation. Relating Schechner's (1988:56) view on performance to the above episode, performance attains its self-realization. The aim is not only a wish to make performance efficacious, but also to use it to change people. However, performance in this situation, yet, according to

Schechner (1988:132), is not a passive mirror of social change, but it is part of the complicated feedback process that creates change.

Court Singers

Another genre of oral performance for the aristocrats is the court singers, who base their performances on oral songs to praise the royalty of the aristocrats, entertain them and their subjects, and ridicule the adversaries of the aristocrats. More often than not, the praises are linked to historical tradition, which focus on expertise in war-fare of the lineage of the aristocrats. However, nowadays that wars and disputes between emirates are no longer practised, emphasis on the praises has shifted to the good leadership qualities of the aristocrats. The mode of communication to the audience has also shifted to the electronic media to conform to change from the traditional, contrary to what Kofoworola and Lateef (1987:79) assert,

> The performing arts groups of the aristocracy perform for the consumption of the aristocracy; the settings of their performances areusually located in certain places, in the presence of particular members of the society and on special ceremonial occasions.

5 FROM PERFORMANCE TO THEATRE AND TO VIDEO FILMS

In 1986, Hubert Ogunde got the mandate from the Federal Government of Nigeria to form a theatre troupe of talented artists with the aim of providing a national theatre company. Ogunde succeeded and the troupe performed at the National Theatre Iganmu-Lagos by providing dances and plays not only in English, the official language, but also in some indigenous languages such as Hausa, Ibo and Yuruba. However, other troupes from other ethnic groups in northern Nigeria such as Afezere (Bauchi and Plateau States) Tera (Gombe State) and Tiv (Benue State) also became vibrant.

Apart from what is considered the national theatre company, some states in northern Nigeria have their cultural and theatre troupes within the auspices of the state's Arts Council. They are mainly concerned with the preservation of conventional modes of performance through annual cultural festival. As Furniss states, "theatricality is also a feature of festivals and court life, as well as a wide variety of cultural events both state sponsored and locally organised" (1996:84). Besides national and state theatre troupes, there are private theatre troupes. They are troupes that are non-governmental and are therefore funded by individuals.

Drama Groups and their Transitions

Between 1980 and 1984, the time which marks the beginning of Kannywood video films in Kano, there abounded drama groups such as the Gyaranya Drama Group, Gwauron Dutse Drama Group and Tumbin Giwa Drama Group. Plays (that were not published) such as, *Hukuma Maganin `Yan Banza* (The Police Arrest the Wayward People) and *Auren Dole* (Forced Marriage) were products of the groups. Among the drama groups, Tumbin Giwa Drama Group and Maitama Sule Drama Group were famous. While Gidado Waziri, a teacher at the then Government College (the present Rumfa College, Kano) founded Tumbin Giwa Drama Group in 1979, Maitama Sule founded Maitama Sule Drama Group. Plays of both groups shifted from stage drama and featured in the Nigeria Television Authority, Kano and also in the State Television Station CTV 67 as television drama particularly during religious festivals like the Eid-el-Fitri and Eid-el-Kabir. In 1984, Tumbin Giwa Drama Group produced a play called *Ma Ji Ma Gani* (We Shall Hear and then See) for NTA, Kano and in 1987 it presented another drama program titled *Jamila da Jamilu* (Jamila and Jamilu).

As for Maitama Sule Drama Group, its first stage theatre took place in 1948. The play was titled *Sarkin Barayi Nomau* (Nomau, the Chief of the Thieves). The play deals with the menace of highway robbery. This group underwent a series of transformations. According to Adamu (2005:9), "the troupe metamorphosed into Kano Drama Troupe and later, perhaps because of the official grants to them from the Treasury, became part of the Kano Native Authority film Unit in 1948". One of its plays, *Bako Raba Dan Gari Kaba* (The Stranger is Merely a Bird of Passage), deals with the British colonial defeat and control of northern Nigeria and the subsequent power struggles and political freedom by Nigerian elites. This development might suggest that a new genre of theatre emerges and starts to be practised or conducted because of the radicalism by some elites who keep on questioning the socio-political system. It is synonymous with what Rubin describes as, "a theatre of social and political commitment, making use of indigenous performative forms in addition to western dialogue drama giving rise to a hybrid theatre created and performed communally" (1997:222).

Theatre groups continue to play their roles as sources of information, education and entertainment for the civil society in general as well as a source of buttressing their civic pride and identities. In addition, the groups serve as training camps for artists, most of whom are aged now. However, for some, their children and wards receive the baton and have become Kannywood video film stars to suggest that not only theatre metamorphoses to Kannywood video films, but the stars also undergo similar shift. Audu Kano, who used to feature in *Karkuzu*, a drama show in the 1980s, is now featuring in Kannywood as a veteran actor. Adamu (2008:10) cites Saratu Gidado, a popular actress in Kannywood video films, who takes up to acting from her father Muhammad Gidado alias Mr. G. As a youth, Mr. G. was an active member of Maitama Sule Drama Group. Other veteran actresses such as Hafsat Sharada and Hajara Usman take on stage drama as amateurs before they shift to achieve a strong reputation for their roles in Kannywood industry. Sharada alias Mai Aya, who passed away on November 17, 2015 was considered as the oldest actress in Kannywood. Her latest video film (done before her death) *Hajiya Babba* (2015) features Chinedu Ikedieze alias Aki, a popular

Nollywood acter. Also, Usman features in many video films such as *Waraka* (2004), *Zaman Gida* (2010), *Rabin Jiki* (2011), *Matar Jami'a* (2013) and *Mazan Ko Matan* (2010). Similarly, Bashir Nayaya, one of the founding members of Ruwan Dare Drama Group in 1969 according to Adamu (2005:11) is now a mentor and veteran in Kannywood industry for acting in video films such as *Bana Bakwai* (2007), *Dijangala* (2008), *Rabuwa* (2008), *Hubbi* (2012), *Gabar Cikin Gida* (2013). This development in Kannywood is practically the same in Nollywood. Stars such as Zab Ejiro, Zack Amata, late Justus Esiri and Lis Benson used to act in different outstanding national drama series: *Ripples*, *Cock Crow at Dawn*, *The Village Headmaster* and *Fortunes* respectively. As the transition from stage drama emerges, the stars in these groups shifted to feature in Nollywood, the Nigerian film industry.

It is worthy to mention that the drama groups remain autonomous groups, but the television stations control the products of their activities - the plays. This indicates that the groups lack control of distribution. Therefore, lack of complete autonomy and the emergence of commercial home video in southern Nigeria spark off the campaign for the need to have the same kind of film industry in northern Nigeria. In 1990, Adamu (2011) posits that the Tumbin Giwa Drama Group became independent and produces what is regarded as the first successful commercial video entitled *Turmin Danya* (1990). The video passed through the process of production by having a written script and a film director in the person of Ibrahim Mandawari. Mandawari used the stars of Tumbin Giwa Drama Group as the basis for the casts in *Turmin Danya* (1990). He considered that they were already familiar with acting. They had no fear of all-eyes-are-on-me syndrome, and shivering behind the camera was no longer a problem. Evidently, these factors influenced their smooth transition from stage to video medium.

Other troupes that are non-governmental and were funded by individuals of note in northern Nigeria in the 80s and 90s were the Parable Repertory Group, Zaria, Kuliya Manta Sabo, Kano, Maitama Sule Group, Kano, Karkuzu Company, Jos, Idon Matambayi, Sokoto, Yautai, Kaduna and Kowace Gauta Ja Ce, Bauchi. It is pertinent to mention that none of these troupes exists anymore today for different reasons. For example, Kowace Gauta Ja Ce, Bauchi split into two in 1996 when Bauchi State was carved into two states, Bauchi and Gombe. The division necessitated the movement of civil workers of Gombe origin to leave Bauchi and work in their new state, Gombe. This development did not only cripple the activities of the troupe, but it also forced the troupe to a standstill. But contrary to this setback, Iyantama's Drama Group metamorphosed into a Kannywood video film production company. Summarily, one could say that, even though some of the non- governmental theatre troupes ceased to function, however, they made an impact on the history, development and metamorphosis of performance into Kannywood video film, as many members of the troupes shifted to the film industry.

Hausa Modern Theatre Tradition to Film Medium

Literary texts in Hausa began to flourish when the Hausa acquired the language skills of reading and writing in Arabic through Muslim scholars in the fourteenth century. But Umaru Balarabe Ahmed (2000:60) argues that even though Islam was formally introduced to Hausa society in the fourteenth century, no Hausa literary text existed before that period of time. Ahmed emphasizes that available evidence of Hausa literary texts dates back to the seventeenth century and these were writings of Wali Dan-Marina and Wali Dan Masani of Katsina which were mainly on religion. It means that written drama was not prominent during early Hausa literary texts. Instead, written poetry receives more attention and it becomes the most established and popular literary genre due to the influence of Islam on Hausa society. Scripted text drama in Hausa made a breakthrough during colonialism with R.M. East *Six Hausa Plays* in 1936. A debut of another Hausa written play was the publication of *Wasan Marafa* by Abubakar Tunau in 1949.

To a greater extent, the plays are a mixture of indigenous forms with foreign theatre tradition adopted by educated Hausa. They deal with general social problems in Hausa society such as child abuse, forced marriage and prostitution. Apart from these texts which have Hausa as their source language, other texts are products of translation into Hausa from English and Arabic sources.

The Impact of School Stage Drama on Film Production

In northern Nigeria, formal schools that offer secular or western education started in 1865 in Lokoja under Bishop Samuel Ajayi Crowther. Later in 1903 other schools were established in Kano and Wusasa near Zaria. In 1922 a college in Katsina was commissioned by Governor of Nigeria (1919 – 1925), Sir Hugh Clifford. The principal of the college was Mr G.A.J Bienemann. Among the teachers were Gerald Power, C.R. Butler and C.E.J Whitting, as Ahmadu Bello (1961:29) explains. After realising that stage drama is very pleasing as well as fascinating in terms of invoking imagination, learning how to express ideas and communicate them, building confidence and making fun, a formal way of achieving these goals emerged in schools as school drama.

The earlier attempts to write drama for stage adaptations in schools, according to Pilaszewicz (1985:228), were undertaken by Aminu Kano as an individual. In 1938 – 1939, while he was still in secondary school, Kano produced plays in which he criticises the exploitation of the ordinary men and challenges the system of the ruling class in northern Nigeria. In the plays *Kai Wane ne a Kasuwar Kano Da Ba Za a Cuce Ka Ba* (Whoever You Might Be, You Will Be Cheated in Kano Market) and *Karya Fure Take Ba Ta `Ya`ya* (A Lie Blooms But Yields No Fruit), he depicts the exploitation of the common man by cruel and unkind merchants and he raises the problem of the excessive taxes levied upon the Hausa rural population. In 1939 – 1941, Kano produced about twenty short plays for use in schools, in which he ridicules some of the old fashion local customs or the conservatism of the older generation as well as the activities of the Native Authority in the system of indirect colonial administration.

Stage Theatre to Television Drama

For the purpose of this study, television drama is more relevant than radio drama. Even though television is more expensive and it requires electricity to operate, most drama groups resolve to television for reaching out to their audience. As such, many Hausa drama shows feature in almost all television stations in states in northern Nigeria. A prominent drama series in the 1960s was *Zaman Duniya Iyawa Ne* (Living Requires

Wisdom), produced by Yusuf Ladan. One of the popular actors in *Zaman Duniya Iyawa Ne* is Usman Baba Fategi. Fategi became autonomous and established his show series called *Samanja Mazan Fama* (Sergeant-major the Struggler) in 1973 which appeared on National Television Authority, Kaduna. The drama centres on the character plays by Fategi himself and demonstrates varieties of circumstances around the military barracks. Fategi's use of language in the drama alone is drama because he imitates a typical recruit or ordinary Nigerian as he or she talks, code mixing English and Hausa. Fategi himself was a soldier in the Nigerian Army during the civil war (1967-1970), so he used that experience in forming the character of *Samanja* (Furnish 1996).

Television continued to be one of the most influential channels for the dissemination of information for the few that could afford it until the 1970s and the 1980s that witnessed enhanced economic and social development: more people particularly civil workers could afford to own television sets in the 70s. This was possible relatively due to the oil boom and its subsequent dividend: a bonus to civil workers called Odoji[10]. In the 80s, more states were curved out hence more television stations were established. To foster and maintain this goodwill by the federal government, more local programmes were added for viewing.

With television sets easily available, coupled with the establishment of more television stations by the federal and some state governments, Hausa media become more available on a daily basis and drama shows became prominent programmes by making a transition to the screen. Among such programmes were *Karambana* and *Kasagi*. While Kasimu Yero handled *Karambana* by preparing the story outlines of each episode and directing the production for television recording, Umaru Danjuma Katsina managed *Kasagi* by preparing the story outlines of the episodes and assisting in its directing. Both Yero and Katsina were the lead characters in each of their respective programmes. *Kasagi* and *Karambana* provide insight into part of what this work is attempting to uncover. While *Kasagi*, on the one hand, contains a further component part that is typical of much theatre – the exposition of particular social

---

10   Udoji is the family name of Jerome Oputa Udoji. He was the Chairman of a panel on Public Service Organization, Management and Remuneration, which General Yakubu Gowon, Nigeria's Military Head of State between 1967 and 1975 constituted. Gowon implemented the salary aspect of the report by giving civil workers bonus that was labeled as Udoji Award or just simply Udoji.

policy issues that require dissemination by the government (Furniss 1996), typical of government programmes that are transformed into video films by Kannywood filmmakers, *Karambana*, on the other hand, depicts a case of cultural transformation as outlined by Koforowola and Lateef (1987:172) thus,

> *Karambana* could be likened to the court jester in the traditional social setting transported into modern social setting. He behaves in all sorts of manner, satirising men of various status in the society in order to purge them of their moral laxity, anti-social practices, misuse and abuse of offices or privileges.

In Sokoto, another television drama series known as *Idon Matambayi* (Eye of the Inquirer) features Bello Abubakar and Muhammad 'Dan'iya as producers. The theme of the drama series focuses on traditional customs and the confrontation between the old and the new. The natives see the emergence and arrival of representatives of modernity from the city such as soldiers and census officials, as well as travelling embodiments of traditional culture: singers, boxers, wrestlers and entertainers of the rural and urban Hausa world. This signifies that, as Furniss maintains "television dramas can have a considerable link to other oral performances in Hausa in addition to new themes relating to issues such as the negative effects of sending female children hawking on streets, rumour circulation, the importance of secular education for male and female children" (Furniss 1996:85).

Theatre and Film Production

Theatre has considerably contributed to the development of Kannywood video films. When the challenges and calls for indigenous Nigerian films became louder, theatre and drama traditions already existed, actors and actresses, the audiences were available as well. The establishment of the Nigerian video film industry in the south of Nigeria that is later on labelled as Nollywood in addition to the films of some earlier talented filmmakers such as Adamu Hallilu and Sadik Abubakar Balewa with their films *Shaihu Umar* (1976) and *Kasarmu Ce* (1991) respectively motivated film production in northern Nigeria in one way or the other. These films served as a challenge in the north whereby some producers, cameramen and artists working with national and state television stations teamed up to display their talents and in a short time, Hausa films begin to appear in markets for sale. Already, Indian and Chinese films were on the program of cinemas (before they were shut down in 2000 in some states in northern Nigeria) which had made an impact by catching the minds of thousands of viewers. Drama groups had produced actors, whose performances did not only succeed in getting available viewers, but they also served as a motivation for establishing individual film production companies.

A significant milestone in the evolution of modern Hausa drama was reached in 1982 with the staging and subsequent publication of Umar Balarabe Ahmed's play, *Amina* (1983). The play focuses on the famous warrior and queen of Zazzau (Zaria), who reigned in the fifteenth century. *Amina* (1983) becomes the first play written in verse in Hausa according to Ahmed (2000:64). It is worthy to mention that some of the written drama books shifted to the screen through conversion into video as feature films. Ahmed's *Amina* (1983) underwent a process of metamorphosis from print to stage. Another example of this kind of metamorphosis is Abubakar Tafawa Balewa's *Shaihu Umar* (1971), a prose, which shifted to a dramatized version with the same title *Shaihu Umar* (1974) by Umaru Ladan and Dexter Lyndersay and finally to a film also titled *Shaihu Umar* (1976), directed by Adamu Halilu. The most striking development was the film *Ruwan Bagaja* (1998), which shifted from orality to literacy and on to electronic processing. As the aforementioned examples show, transformations involved orality and literacy, I uphold the argument of Walter J. Ong (1982:15) that "literacy is absolutely necessary for the development not only of science but also of history, philosophy, explicative understanding of literature and of any art, and indeed for the explanation of language (including oral speech) itself". Therefore, oral culture produces the print culture and the subsequent electronic culture which builds on both orality and written literature.

Conclusion

Modification is manifest in Hausa theatre that makes an impact as a source of electronic media, especially the video film industry. As the case was, theatre events in indigenous Hausa and African settings in general were meant to be watched by the entire community or by a general public, and the venue was usually an open space. However, an influence of Western culture is manifest. On one hand, theatre has shifted from the indigenous open spaces to modern stages such as the theatre halls, for instance the Multi-purpose Hall and Theatre Hall in Bauchi, which are used as venues for performances. On the other hand, Hausa actors and actresses in drama groups gradually have realized that they can make a video coverage of their performances and thus preserve it for a later viewing. This realization has led to the transportation of Hausa drama and the subsequent rise of Kannywood industry that produces Kannywood video film which is now a popular means of entertainment in both Hausa urban and rural areas of northern Nigeria and other African countries. Not only is the source (theatre) involved in the transformation, but also the medium of communication, the Hausa language - the language of the video films. The new medium is witnessed by urbanism to suggest a shift from the simple enactments of the earlier Hausa theatre which depicted Hausa traditionalism to modern hybrid that shows the impact of technology. Moreover, the dialogues move from monolingualism to ones characterized by code switching from Hausa to English to reflect the characters' acquired knowledge of urban *Engausa*[11] More so, the indigenous theatre does not only metamorphose into television shows and various varieties of films, but the contents also depict radical changes to reflect existing happenings. Thus, an exploration into the films along with analysis is necessary in order to investigate the different forms of transformations that are manifested through Kannywood video films.

---

11 *Engausa* is an acronym coined from ENGlish and hAUSA. It refers to the verbal speech that consists both English and Hausa words due to either code switching or code mixing or both. It could be regarded as a hybridized Hausa often spoken by urban dwellers.

6 MEMORY AND PERFORMANCE IN KANNYWOOD FILMS

This chapter analyzes six selected video films. Film analysis is primarily about making claims on the film's meaning using proof from the film. It entails how a film is put together and how the narrative is constructed (Ryan & Lenos 2012:28). Therefore, the selected video films are *Ruwan Bagaja* (1998) directed by Iliyasu Abdulmumini, *Sangaya* (2000) directed by Aminu Muhammad Sabo, and *Borin Ibro* (2008) directed by Auwal Y. Abdullahi. Others are *Tashe* (2010) directed by Hamisu Yusuf. *Fulani* (2012) directed by Mu''azzam Idi Yari, and *Karen Bana* (2013) directed by Falalu A. Dorayi. The video films integrate adaptations of folktales and reenactment of oral performance events. However, the folktales and performances depicted on screen might show some differences from the original one that the screen narrative is about. As Gehrmann explains, each form of orature that is transformed (in her case into a written form) loses the particular character of the oral performance situation (2005:158). The aim of this analysis is to explore the changes that are encountered in the selected video films, as they move from one medium to another.

Folktale Video Film: *Ruwan Bagaja* (Water for Cure)

Content of *Ruwan Bagaja*

The video film *Ruwan Bagaja*[12] is about a polygamous man whose two wives. Hama, played by Maryam Tahir, and Larai, played by Yahanasu Sani, do not enjoy equal treatment. He loves Larai more than Hama and the love extends to her daughter. The extreme dislike towards Hama extends to her daughter as well. While Hama does domestic work and takes the role of a maid at the detriment of her marriage, her co-wife Larai

---

12 Although the video film *Ruwan Bagaja* (1998) bears the same title with Abubakar Imam's fiction novel also *Ruwan Bagaja* (1939), in this book, consideration is only on the video film, not Imam''s novel of the same title, even though the two are primarily true to folktale as their sources.

does no domestic work, but functions as the mistress of the house. Each of them fulfills a function and role which are the fundamental components of the underlying folktale. Therefore, the function and role of each character is presented in terms of their significance for the plotline's course of action. Both Hama and Larai, the two principal characters and their acts are seen in relation to each other and to the video film as a whole, thus expressing the importance of their functions to the general development of the plot.

A family row erupts to bring about tension in the video film after Larai's daughter, played by Sadiya Mohammed, bed-wets while sleeping at night. In the morning, Hama''s daughter, rather than the culprit, is accused of bed-wetting. Therefore, she is ordered to go and wash the *kirgi* (tanned cowhide used as bed sheet) in river *Bagaja* which is very far and difficult to reach. She obeys the order and goes out in search of *ruwan bagaja* (water of cure). During the search, she encounters many situations that are horrifying, yet she endures and continues her ordeal. When she comes to a river, she sings with humble and soft words along with thrilling rhythms to inquire if that is river *bagaja*.

After intensive search, she finds river *bagaja*, washes the bed sheets, and obeys the instructions given to her. Eventually, she finds miraculous favor and returns home in triumphant entry: on horse with escorts, drumming and musical beats befitting a princess. Having seen Hama and her daughter in this honor, Larai instructs her daughter to bed-wet in order to repeat the cycle. But as she has been pampered by their parents, hence she has a rude character. Consequently, when she goes to the river to wash the bed sheets she is impolite. As a result, she comes back home on a donkey along with lepers as escorts and together with her mother they continue to live in poverty for the rest of their lives.

Folktale across Different Media

While I consider what Sherman refers to as the folkloric films (2007:2), I also take the concept of performance into account that suggests an aesthetically marked and heightened mode of communication, framed in a special way and put on display for an audience (Bauman 1992:41). Invariably, Bauman''s approach suggests shifting of action from one medium to another and in the case of this work, from arena to screen. Oral performance in public and performance on screen basically involve linguistic signs involving facial expressions such as eye contact, blinking, raised eyebrows, widened eyes and gaping mouth, squeezed eyebrows and display of teeth. However, performance on screen is different from performance in the arena because it involves audio-visual and fixed images are created through the use of the camera, whose main function is to capture and represent the actions in performance in arena in a different medium, namely video film. The second point of departure is from the two processes of communication. The participants that are involved in the process of communication in the oral performance in the arena consist of the performers and audience. But those who are involved in the performance on screen are the characters and viewers, whereas the direct exchange between oral performer and public is crucial for any oral performance event. The product of the work of the filmmakers and characters are processed in a video film for everyone to view. Evidently, as the case is there is a new element not only from the oral to the written, but from the oral to the technical audio-visual media as well. Folktale, for instance, that once emerged as authentic, is transformed through convergence of folktale and film. The concept of how folktale performance is keyed as an integral component is also affected. Traditionally, each community made use of a structured set of distinctive special formulas that would be understood as folktale within that community (Bauman, 1992:45). Bauman is supported by Ahmad (1997:18) in this respect as he enumerates how in Hausa, a folktale starts and ends. This traditional pattern key among narrator and audience constitutes a breach of a generic conventional order and injects a change in the video film. For the director, that infringement of order will not deter the flow of the story, as the most essential is the content of the story. Therefore, it becomes clear that transportation of performance from one medium to another, as Joubert (2004:94) explains, involves the interplay of information among different media of mixed sign systems. In the same vein, if performance based video films are considered as reinterpretation and rendition of the world around the filmmakers, then it is evident that the performances in video films must be rendered erratic, as no two performances are ever exactly the same. Similarly, Krings (2010:80) in his study of localization of Nigerian video films in Tanzania posits that each medium has its own intrinsic qualities. What are some of the likely changes when one genre is passed through different media? This question leads to the issue of metamorphosis of performance, which is the focus of this work.

The Dynamics and Flexibility of *Ruwan Bagaja*

The folktale *Ruwan Bagaja* has fictional characters and settings. But when Iliyasu Abdulmumini decides to film *Ruwan Bagaja*, fictional characters and locations such as Hama, Larai, the house and the river respectively become visually mimetic of real-life names and locations. Even though it is not a documentary, it is highly mimetic of reality, while it is not reality as such.

The shift from the folktale *Ruwan Bagaja* to video film is noticeable. Shift is pervasive in the enumeration of traditional features in the video film, synonymous to what Blackford (2007:76) considers the dynamic, modern storytelling of popular film. In this sense, technology threatens the authority of the storyteller and brings about her obsolescence. The traditional Hausa old woman and *amarya* (bride) involved in folktale as narrators do not reclaim their status in the video film. They do not survive as storytellers, or keepers of memory, and those who express morality for children in the present. Evidently, not only the content of the folktale is affected, but also, there is a change in the way of accessing it. The storyteller in folktale is not only in direct contact with his or her audience, but s/he is also able to adjust his or her delivery to the audience''s reactions spontaneously. The dialogue takes place between the storyteller and the audience who normally stand or sit around the performer. As Wynchank (1994:13) suggests, "the audience strongly react, respond to questions, join in refrains, in brief, they participate in the recounting. On the contrary, a film is made once, and for all types of audience, and can be viewed by anyone at any moment. Obviously, dialogue does not take place literally between them, for the filmmaker cannot adjust his or her narration to the changes of mood of his or her audience". It means that the video film changes the pattern of its use from a group of children venue for listening time in the terrace with an old woman or bride to a family to the viewing situation in front of a television that can be communal or individual. By inference, now the viewer is confined to the video medium with its constant flow of images. On one hand, the viewer of the video film has an advantage from the opportunity to see images of the characters and hear what they say as well, unlike in folktale performance where the issue of the imagination of the listeners is primarily essential.

The audience listening to a storyteller recounting his or her tale can only make use of their imagination to see the characters and actions. In contrast, according to Wynchank (1994:14), "films show images which give the illusion of reality, leaving very little to the imagination of the spectators […] Images can kill the imagination". Hence, the viewers lose some qualities of the folktale. By implication, the folktale suffers a loss because of the almost complete disappearance of the emotional color which comes from the narrator"s gestures and mimicry, as well as the intonation of her own voice and her imitation of the voices of the characters. It is replaced by the actors'' capabilities to display emotions. This work finds the video film coming of age to demonstrate the power of transformation for the folktale in order to tally with time.

There is a shift from the traditional folkloric idea of magical transformation to the depiction of an appearance of real and physical object. For example, when Zainab and Sadiya break eggs on different occasions, viewers see different things coming to life from the eggs. The traditional feature of magical power in the folktale comes to the video film and coexists with the real and physical object and takes hybrid form which reflects local ambivalence towards globalization. Not only that, the folktale itself can be defined by its structure of journey and metamorphosis. The two protagonists, Zainab and Sadiya undergo significant transformations as a reward for perseverance and obedience as opposed to laziness and insolence.

While the performative approach to folktales has been concerned with the motifs of folktales (Peterson, 2007:94), in the video film, emphasis is put on the way narrative and performance conventions are modified to meet a specific demand. For example, at the same time when the narrative is going on, viewers hear sound in the form of music. The music as the case is does not only increase the intensity of the film immensely, but it also shows the technical means through which the audio and visual worlds come together in film. More often than not, the words in the music describe feelings and bring much more emotion on the screen than the dialogue alone. The use of sound has changed over time to include the use of image in patterned ways. The folktale in video film is thus made possible by the capacity of the local film industries to appropriate local images, transform them, and circulate them across ever-wider routes of distribution compared to folktale as oral performance.

Set in a rural area, *Ruwan Bagaja* commences with an on-screen image of a typical traditional compound. The compound has two identical mud huts and it is inhabited by one family. The compound as a space is only imagined by the listener of the folktale, now it is made publicly visible. In this case, as Adamu (2010:67) suggests, the secret of the Muslim Hausa female conjugal domain is uncovered or it is not kept away from exposure by the filmmaker. A point of shift from folktale to video film is encountered from the director's choice of names for the two principal rivals in the video film. The video film shows a departure from the traditional use of the names Mowa and Bora. On the contrary, the names Hama and Larai are used, but without any special significance. But the names Mowa and Bora on the one hand have peculiar importance in the folktale as they signify the level of love, care and concern each wife gets from their polygamous husband. While Mowa has the affection of their husband, Bora is treated by their husband with disaffection.

Although the compound depicts a traditional set-up, the video film showcases a radical departure from the traditional extended family to depict a more contemporary family of three, comprising a man and his two wives. Even though the man is a polygamist, throughout the video film, the family increases to only five members when each of the two wives delivers a baby girl. In respect of thematic emphasis, the video film explores polygamy in a traditional Hausa setting. It focuses on the unbalanced love a wife that is not a favorite of her husband experiences from him and the type of slanderous allegations she encounters from her co-wife. Viewers see Hama actively involved in preparing food, as is expected, for her husband to eat on arrival from hard work on the farm. But she encounters disappointment; as her husband returns, he goes straight to Larai and the camera captures them sitting down discussing amicably. To make things worse for Hama, her rival Larai makes false allegations against her. While there is emphasis on the representation of *kishi* (envy, jealousy) in this scene, my focus is on the manifestation of shift from the traditional norm of behavior. In the traditional environment, a wife does not express her feelings freely to her husband. Larai does not only report Hama to their husband, but she also does that while sitting very close to him without the traditional norm of *kunya*. Her use of language is a shift from what Newman and Gimba (1998: IV) explain about the expressive function of language. According to them, expression should go in agreement with the social and linguistic conventions of the culture. However, Larai seems to tell the viewers that it is high time they departed from the conservative norm that makes them die in silence under the cover of *kunya* (shame). She does not only draw their attention to the modern way in which spouses come very close to each other, but she also depicts that the closest is always the dearest, hence she is the *mowa*. Although their family is portrayed as a divided one, one part of the family cares for each other (Larai has the concern of her husband). This spirit of care is juxtaposed with the non-affectionate condition in which Hama finds her relationship with her husband. The way Larai and her husband are foregrounded in the video film's composition informs the viewer of the type of relationship that exists between husband and wife in modernized and globalized societies and it is beginning to have relevance in a society enshrined by traditional norms. By implication, this situation is more valuable as Larai and her husband are placed at the center of the frame, while Hama is placed in the lower part of the screen. This kind of arrangement which the director employs agrees with what Ryan and Lenos (2012:38) say about what a film is consist of. According to them, "filmmakers usually assign greater importance or value to characters who are centered within the frame or who are located in the upper half of the image".

Ruwan Bagaja does not only depict the character's rise from stagnation to stardom and vice versa, but it also depicts a change in its source. In addition to the video film's source, which is folktale performance, the director incorporates yet another live musical performance involving boys and girls at night in an arena. It is a diversification and change employed by the director to explore more varieties. At that moment, he employs a pleasant or amusing activity that takes the attention of viewers away from the tension in the polygamous family by incorporating entertainment (dancing) in addition to the perspective of morality in the folktale. While the girls sing and dance, the boys admire them thus suggesting to viewers a shift from traditional to popular culture. However, viewers do not see the musicians. They only hear non-synchronous music by means of automatic dialogue replacement (ADR). Its incorporation signifies that folktale in video film like *Ruwan Bagaja* constitutes a modern genre based on appropriation of global musical genre. The music does not only urge the dancers (the girls) to keep on rejoicing, but it also persuades them to dance in a village square, as the chorus says, *'yan mata mu dinga murna da rawa a dandali* (girls, let us keep on rejoicing and dancing at the arena). This development does not only represent a cultural change, but it also shows a peaceful protest by the girls, who want to get involved in open social activities even at the height of restrictions based on ideological differences.

Ruwan Bagaja as a video film has made an effect on viewers because it serves as a means of recalling the old tradition. Viewers recall and see the past in a new medium. However, the new medium allows them access to the past when they want, compared to the time when they get access to folktales only at the discretion of the storyteller. The new medium simplifies a combination of genres and allows their movements without necessarily requiring viewers to form mental pictures. For example, the film''s director moves away from narration to undergo a particular performance genre, involving the protagonist in a characteristic manner thus:

> Ko kai ne ruwan bagaja
>
> Ko ba kai ba ruwan bagaja
>
> Domin ƙirgi aka aiko ni
>
> In zo in wanke a ruwan bagaja (*Ruwan Bagaja* 00:58:56 minutes)

Although the above song is a side issue and not a main issue in the video film it has significance in the video film and in this work in particular. It helps in accomplishing one of the messages in the video films, especially the moralistic aspect: obeying the required instruction. Secondly, it helps in realizing one of the functions of song in video films. It creates a specific emotion in relation to the situation which Zainab depicts on screen. Her mood while singing the song expresses her feelings of desperation to get out of depression, making the song to participate in human emotions, particularly sadness. It manifests a distinction between her and the audience. The director employs an interplay and overlap of narrative and performative forms thereby exhibiting aesthetics of narrative performance. Zainab the actress adjusts the quality and energy of her gesture, voice and action to communicate her shifting desires and her performance is keyed to the narrative which provides musical score for the film''s rising and falling action. The energy and quality of her movements and vocal expressions are equally important. Her performance which viewers see (compared to when they only hear it transmitted through the storyteller) contributes to the mood or feeling conveyed by the director, thereby corresponding to the Hausa proverb, *gani ya kori ji* (seeing is believing) which is a major aspect of change in the new medium that this work is discussing. The video film in this sense of change involves a narrative shift from ordinary speaking into performance that involves use of gestures and rhythmical language, as well as the use of instrumental accompaniment, interspersing prose with songs. While viewers hear the song on screen, the incorporation of musical instruments is off screen. Apart from emphasis on shift from narration to performance, there is also emphasis on metamorphosis in the video film''s characters. Zainab and her mother take a new role. They cease to be what they were: rejected daughter and mother. Now they act in a more dignified status compared to princess and queen. In a way their situations serve to conform to folktale characters fulfilling roles, in their case the roles of heroine. Taking a new role qualifies them to find honor and respect where they were least expected. They continue to live in peace and in wealth. This marks the beginning of a turning point in their lives. What suggests an aesthetically marked and heightened mode of communication to explore metamorphosis for the audience is the dramatic twist. In the beginning Hama and Zainab, her daughter, are doomed to outright poverty with no hope of a brighter future. In line with the happy ending of the folktale, but expanded through more showing pictures (instead of the condensed telling by the oral performer) they turn out to be in control of wealth, courtesy of the things the girl brings back home from her travels in search of *ruwan bagaja*.

The video film is marked by a change in equilibrium compared to the folktale. It moves towards the direction of recapturing the feelings of viewers more than in the folktale. Although there is binary construction already present in the folktale, rather, in the video film it is expanded, amplified and strengthened. The director emphasizes more on binary contradiction by affording the viewers to see actions and their consequences, such as pursuit and rescue, struggle and victory between Hama and Larai on one hand and between their daughters on the other hand. Consequently, they see a distribution of characters and their behavior into two mutually exclusive categories: Sadiya as a rude character is discourteous or impolite. She displays behavior completely opposite of her sister's. The director in this scene employs free-floating physical gestures in the role Sadiya plays to portray her as a rude character. He amplifies her vocal expressions to speak loud whenever she requests to break an egg as instructed. This development helps to convey her arrogant thoughts and emotions to the audience thereby creating a mood and depicting a shift from the traditional norm of *ladabi da biyayya* (respect and obedience), behavior expected of any child. To make sure the audience gets the message, he further uses a close-up shot to show her coming back home on a donkey along with lepers as escorts in addition to setting the camera to follow her with her entourage for a long distance walk, as she and her mother continue to live in poverty for the rest of their lives. The video film is thus marked by a reversal of roles in which it presents Larai and her daughter as false heroines. This concurs with the underlying morality of the folktale, but is depicted in more detail in the film through an amplification of the plot. It would be right to say that Abdulmumini's *Ruwan Bagaja* is an example of a typical heroic narrative. It tells a story of an individual who overcomes a threat in her life in a household, which she does not only live in, but belongs to as a bona fide heir. In the course of this, viewers see Zainab (Hama's daughter) as she embraces the spirit of cultural norms, which they too partake in. At the same time, they see Sadiya (Larai's daughter), the villain, breaking cultural norms by violating one particular basic cultural rule such as respect, and predictably, at the end, she descends while the heroic abider of cultural norms triumphs. The filmmaker adopts the genre of the folktale and transforms it into a full-fledged film through media appropriation. He still proves the same moralistic stance as the folktale does.

Constructively, the narratives in *Ruwan Bagaja* involve progressive movement from a negative to a positive condition for the heroine (and decline for the villain). The protagonist emerges from a state of weakness to various situations of transformation, rebirth, strength and freedom, as she rises from a condition of impasse to that of accolade. She is accused of bed-wetting, and during the course of the plotlines she gets instructions on how to get *ruwan bagaja* to wash the bed sheet and how not to make a mistake in getting it. The success in achieving this task is a feature of a character transformation, a passage from incapability to ability.

Abdulmumini's *Ruwan Bagaja* is thus a transformation of folktale performance, which is presented from the perspective of traditional tale after supper. As it is the practice, children request an old woman or bride to tell them stories during an evening of relaxation, in which the woman or bride takes the role of narrator and tells the story. However, the video film departs from this technique by not maintaining a single narrator. Rather, all the characters partake in the narratives repeatedly. This work considers that the departure and the new narrative employed have to do with the change in medium and the director's aim of reinforcing the basic norms of culture and struggle. For example, viewers easily realize the repetition of camera, and the repetition in movements of setting up a journey in search of *ruwan bagaja* and coming back home by both Hama and Larai's daughters, to suggest an act that is not only basic, but continuous in human endeavors. Such are events people perform to themselves that evoke not only harmonious but also collective responses according to a familiar world-view. Their aesthetic standards are now interpreted in terms of a new frame of reference. The new medium does not only explore maximum interpretation, but also manifests the significance and use of some symbolic elements and their impact on society and culture. The culture of one man marrying more than one wife is not only a case of polygamy, but it also discusses the kind of changes encountered between husband and wives in matrimonial homes. Although it is not mentioned in the video film, yet it gives the impression that such biased treatment nowadays extends between the offspring of the wives, as it is noticeable in contemporary situations with regard to the minimal cordial relationship between *'yan uba* (step brothers) in the society. In comparison to this, the video film shifts to the issue of child upbringing and the culture of patience, especially for a woman whose husband does not regard her with favor. Therefore, as a reward for obedience, Zainab survives the obstacles in her travail at *ruwan bagaja* and she is made to have a change as seen on screen.

Furthermore, going beyond the images on screen, there is the change in the concept of water as a symbol in the video film. Neatness in the context of the film is not only a process of removing dirt or urine from the *ƙirgi* (bed sheet) as in the folktale. While the folktale emphasizes neatness of only the outer part of man, the video film showcases change to include also the purification of the heart: the inner part of man. As the young girls (Zainab and Sadiya) go to get water, it implies that water does not only clear dirt, but it also takes it away to an unknown destination. In the course of getting water to be neat, the girls undergo series of difficult situations and challenges. In essence, they encounter many obstacles on the way. This situation indicates a new approach to life which suggests that for someone to be pure in heart he or she is bound to face temptations to make him or her remain impure. But when he or she shows perseverance, he or she will see reward, as Zainab comes back home changed and triumphant after a successful cleansing to depict a new concept that suggests cleanliness is next to godliness compared to bed-wetting, which has a stigma attached to it. It is considered a bad habit and in real life situation, particularly in Hausa society, if a child persists in doing it, he/she is ridiculed by his/her peer group using a song. However, the song is no longer a popular children song today. Therefore, this work considers the present unpopularity of the song as a justification of cultural shift today. However, let me quote it in full length.

Amalala mai fitsarin kwance

Ya tsulla ya daɗa tsulawa

Da ya tsula sai da ya kai Barno

Amalala (2010) (A bed-wetter) directed by Umar Jalo exists to support my claim.

In folktale, audience does not see characters and their actions. They can only imagine the trends of events through repetition, eye contact, gesture and mime to ensure that they follow and comprehend the plot because folktale is abstract. So therefore, someone who hears only the folktale *Ruwan Bagaja* uses his or her own sense of imagination to create images in his/her mind But someone who has trans-media experience by hearing the folktale and watching the video film may have cause to trace the video film's trajectory across different media and can notice a mark of metamorphosis. For example, the scene of *cinya da kare* (thigh and dog) in the folktale where the protagonist meets the Thigh and the Dog in a hut beside river *bagaja* before she washes the bed-sheet is cut off in the video film. On one hand, such a cut can reduce the flow of the content and as a result essential information may not be absorbed. On the other hand, there is the need to deal with situations in a more practical way and according to what is real or possible, from the filmmaker's perspective. In other words, the more realistic genre of the film shifts away from the magical elements which are inherent in the folktale genre - this counts for this particular film, other films may well use magical elements and create surreal (false) images through montage techniques. Therefore, the director cuts off actions which are imagined rather than visualized such as non-humans taking up the qualities and characteristics of humans like talking, despite the fact that the present era of technological advancement has made animation in video films possible. Stylistic hybridization draws the viewer's attention to distinguish between the real and imagined events. It prompts participation in the search for implicit or connotative meanings of the images represented. Notwithstanding, skipping the scene makes the video film more realistic.

In the context of this work, metamorphosis does not only concern the medial channels of transmission, but it also involves the methods of preservation and networking. *Ruwan Bagaja* as a folktale undergoes a change from what is known as *adabin baka* in Hausa literature. Orality, folktale's main characteristic, has now witnessed a shift to electronic media comprising of not only sound, but a combination of sound and image. In the words of Anny Wynchank (1994:13), "an orality which is mechanically transmitted, deferred in time and space, where the new media find their place". And viewers see the correlation between the speech they hear from characters and their moving lips. Characters in the video film manifest attitudes in the positive and negative perspectives with considerable shift. For example, horse riding, drumming, music, escorts and perfume in the video film do not only maintain the traditional norm of royalty, but they also include the norm of obedience in an upper class in contemporary society. On the other hand, visually displayed negative elements such as leprosy, flies, insects and riding on donkey provide the impetus for a shift in attitudes to include not only the cultural stigma regarding rudeness and disobedience, but also the poverty struck social conditions that are looked at contemptuously and negatively in the society.

Analysis of *Sangaya* (2000) (Sangaya)

Content of *Sangaya* (2000)

The video film *Sangaya* is set in a palace. The plotline depicts Zubaina, played by Fati Mohammed, as the protagonist who encounters maltreatment from both the maids and the prince. She is subjected to constant domestic work, the type endowed to slaves. She lacks freedom even among fellow maids. Apparently, *Sangaya* shows Zubaina in ambivalent circumstances such as the state of hatred and love, commoner and nobility. These situations are uncovered and made visible, as she experiences a change of status that culminates in a turning point. To achieve this, she performs an act of trick through concealing her identity to the prince, thus enabling her to marry him, which metamorphoses her status, as she eventually attains royalty.

Elements of Metamorphosis of Status

Viewers see the list of production crew moving on screen simultaneously with an off-screen soundtrack of flute and drums. As the soundtrack music subsides, a close up shot of a large grand decorated house (palace) appears. The house fades away for Goggo, a senior maid, who appears on screen treating a maid scornfully, even though the maid, who is the protagonist will later metamorphose and undergo a change from inhumane to humane condition. In accomplishing the perspective of change in status, the director sets the video film in a palace, where there is hierarchy, and uses close and distant shots on both the interior and exterior of the settings. This enables the viewers to experience not only the tension of Tabawa and Zubaina's personal trauma, but it also enables the viewers to encounter with the liminal stage of Tabawa and Zubaina's personal life. Zubaina as a role character with her mother Tabawa have no iota of favor in the palace. As a mother and an elder, culture demands that Tabawa rceives a good opinion of her character and ideas by the younger ones. The maids are not supposed to do things which she would not like or would consider wrong. On the contrary, the video film depicts a departure from an established cultural norm of respect and mutually supportive relationship. This kind of cultural change is realized when a fellow maid accuses Tabawa of stealing sorghum floor meant to prepare pap for the king. In a close up shot, the camera captures the accuser's face as she speaks. It disgusts and dehumanizes the character of an innocent old woman, as the matter does not end as mere speculation and accusation. It includes abuses, scolding and all sorts of maltreatment besides the subsequent strong stigma attached to theft. The director amplifies the sound above normal dialogue and viewers hear loud speech, thereby evoking into the minds of viewers the kind of mood: extreme anger and contempt from the character. This development indicates that the story suffers an immeasurable change due to the almost complete disappearance of the emotional color which comes from the storyteller's gesture and mimicry, as well as the intonation of her voice and the imitation of the voices of the characters. In place of a song by the storyteller, viewers hear an interlude of soundtrack music and a sudden appearance of a woman believed to be *aljana* (spirit) in what is called character transformation. This is a filmic device in which A'isha 'Dankano changes into a spirit in order to show an act of transformation. Her role in the video film does not only communicate to the audience the existence of spirits as evident in *bori* cult, but also shows the role of manipulation for cultural change. In the traditional belief, spirits are only felt. The video film showcases a change in this kind of belief. It is often said that to see is to believe, as such viewers' conception about spirits is reinforced. More so, Zubaina's problems are solved as a result of her encounters with the spirit. Therefore, it is possible that the video film postulates change in people's concept and allegiance to the sorcerers and herbalists. Practically, these days, a lot of people go to the shrines to engage the services of sorcerers and herbalists for whatever they intend to do. The video film fashions people's attitudes to achievements. Ironically, the society upholds and proclaims religion whereby people go to churches and mosques to observe religious rites on one hand, and on the other hand, the same people indulge in acts contrary to religion by consulting sorcerers and herbalists.

Transition From Abstract Images to Physical Events

Characteristically, orature is not only involved in repetition, but it also often involves digression by the narrator to develop a point before coming back to the original narration. Comparatively, the video film presents a non digressive and complete narration. This development enhances viewing and makes it more attractive compared to orature. The device is more valuable for disclosing the background of the characters or events that do not only influence the plot, but they also seem to be extraneous diversions from the plot. It is through the device of non digressive narration as requested by the spirit that Tabawa's background and social status are uncovered as the audience comes to know that both she and her daughter are undergoing a traumatizing situation. In a close up shot, Tabawa is seen gasping for breath. And when she says to Zubaina, "Tell the woman that I am no more and I adjure you to hold on to her" (*Sangaya* 00:07:16 minutes), she is about to die. Naturally, for any living creature there are two opposing moments of life and death. Each point in time has a peculiar cultural value associated with it. At the time someone is born, which marks the beginning of life, by tradition it is a moment of celebration. And death, which marks the end of life, is characterized by mourning. On the contrary, the video film depicts a departure from this cultural value, as the maids assault Zubaina. It is not only un-cultural, but it is also inhuman to intimidate someone who grieves. Evidently, the video film shows that instead of condolence befitting a bereaved person as culture demands, the maids mock Zubaina. They do not show any concern for the death of her mother. To them, death has ceased to be fearful, therefore they do not show any sign of grief. This development is a misdemeanor, which insinuates moral decadence in the society to suggest that death is losing its characteristics of being fearsome. Nowadays during mourning, people are seen discussing politics, sports and they are also laughing at the top of their voices to indicate that death is no longer a new thing. It hits almost every family. To capture the manifestation of the change in cultural values as exemplified by the maids, the cameraman employs the long shot. Framed in this manner, he eschews the close up for long shot. This technique enables the viewers to see a close view of the nature of the shift expedient by the maids as they interact to deal with Zubaina to represent the distribution of the shift in the society.

A continuing aesthetic aspect of change from traditional to contemporary is seen through long, intercept frames of characters as employed by the cameraman. What the camera captures manifests what it is designed to do. Its main function is to make a latent image. After suitable processing and photography technique, the image is then transformed to a usable image and sequence of images. In this sense, it is clear that, the role of tradition in the context of change is not only well-known, but also a continuing phenomenon even before the emergence of video film in northern Nigeria. Furniss, according to Kaschula (2001:XIV), shows how Hausa oral poetry has been absorbed into contemporary popular culture in Nigeria, thereby entrenching or establishing the role of the poet as a socio-political commentator. This is one important area that depicts metamorphosis courtesy of technology. The metamorphosis within the tradition and how this allows to operate in a contemporary environment remains a primary focus for this analysis.

Looking at *Sangaya*, it is clearly noticeable that the abstract nature of orality is overpowered by technology and has witnessed a shift through the application of the camera. As Nagib (2001:102) asserts, "African film in general should cease to be understood only for its inefficient economy and technical qualities". Dasylva (2001:182)) agrees with Nagib in this respect, as he explains that "in Nigeria and in fact Africa, both the context and text of oral literature have had to cope with the challenges of modernity and survival through a series of transformation over the years". Ogaga Okuyade (2014:XXIX) further explains that oral adaptation in a written text has artistically widened the limit of our knowledge on the oral / written interface of African literature. Evidently, oral tradition has been a source of rhetorical device for African writers, as it helps to enhance the structural designs of the written text, the concept which Okuyade has described as "aesthetic metamorphosis or transformation".

Similarly, Anny Wynchank (1994:13) recounts how cinema has been the transmitter of oral tradition, but in a much broader sense. Thus the camera does not only capture images, but the images are also framed in different forms such as quick, slow and tilted. Its expressions represent what the filmmaker wants to achieve. In the case of the video film under review, the director succeeds in representing an example of monarchic rule in traditional society. The arrival of the prince and his entourage disappears off screen and the king and the queen appear on screen. In a long shot, the camera captures the king and the queen in a heart to heart discussion to show a modern style of close dialogue compared to the traditional manner of dialogue far away in space, especially between couples in traditional Hausa/Fulani society. More importantly, the video film enumerates a departure from the traditional form of marriage known as *auren dangi.·* More often than not, this type of marriage causes problems between relatives. Normally, the couples are related by blood, and whenever there is a matrimonial problem between them, it proceeds to involve other relations in the wider family.

In general, repetition is more present in oral narrative than in films. However, repetition of events is a common structural strategy used in *Sangaya* video film as a variable element. As Ahmed (1997:67) asserts, "a skillful performer (in my case filmmaker) adds details, descriptions, songs and gestures whereas a less talented one includes little". The filmmaker makes Zubaina to evolve, as she gradually changes and develops into a different person over a period of time. Having the proficiency to transform herself gives more information about her as the film's character and the events surrounding her, and thus allows the viewers to see her encountering a set of tasks or challenges. For example, as she goes to meet the spirit repeatedly, the spirit's transformation into human form to speak to her takes pre-eminence, as she uses a plural of majesty and honour to speak.

Ni ba mutum ba ce ba.

Ni baiwa ce ta Allah.

Don mu a ɓoye muke.

I am not a human being.

I am a servant of God

Because we are hidden (*Sangaya* 00: 07:16 minutes)

The spirit uses the first person singular *ni* (I) twice and the first person plural *mu* (we) to introduce herself to Zubaina. The use of the first person plural by a speaker to refer to himself or herself as an individual, as used by the spirit signifies a change from human to super human. It is not unlikely that in contemporary speeches, the aristocrats use a similar speech act to lessen their powers over the masses and to curtail the use of veto powers, as freedom of speech and human rights are famous operative opium for the masses in the modern time. Therefore, the mix up of the pronouns means that the spirit is ordinary as she appears on screen. She is also authoritative as she asks Zubaina her problems and gives her instructions on what she has to do. The belief in communication between spirits and humans is discerned through her realistic and practical appearance by means of the manipulation of the camera. The video film is endowed with repetition due to the influence of oral transmission, which places stronger demands on comprehension. However, a change of role and a turning point are condensed through character transformation as a technique in film. For the video film to arrive at the message, Zubaina needs to change and evolve. A while ago, viewers saw her as a wretched child in sackcloth, but later she is somebody else: Azumi in brand new cloth. This development results into deception, one of the actions which Ryan and Lenos (2012:123) posit. In their words, the villain attempts to deceive his victim by using persuasion, magic, or deception. Evidently, Maina is deceived by Zubaina when he meets her on the way back home. She disguises herself to begin an untimely conversation of youthful friendship that matures into courtship. On a symbolic level, this represents the situation nowadays, especially when some intending couples do not show their real characters. More often than not, they claim to be what they are not regarding both material wealth and reputation. They may be wolves in the skin of sheep. They prove to be innocent, but when the going gets tough, they reveal their original colors and attitudes to life. This is similar to a characteristic of performance especially when a performer wears special costumes and disguises himself or herself, the audience is skeptical about his personality. In the same vein, Zubaina conceals her identity. She introduces herself as Azumi and Fulani by origin. She is conscious of her change. But, Maina does not notice the transformation. To him, he is meeting a lady he has never met. Viewers see him staring at a lady from angle to angle and moving round her, as she stands still while an interlude of music plays. The music does not fade away when viewers hear what Maina says to the lady, *"Ni sunana Maina"* (as for me, my name is Maina) (*Sangaya* 00:33:06 minutes). He chooses to use the emphatic pronoun *ni* (I) to introduce himself to show his status as the prince, otherwise, he would have said *sunana Maina* (my name is Maina). The director is able to combine the soundtrack and the dialogue together without making viewers carried away. The viewers are supposed to hear ambient sounds like tweet or chirp of birds because the setting is a footpath in the forest, but there is no distraction, as the director is able to contain the problem. He conforms to selectivity and allows only the diegesis-relevant voices and sounds to be heard.

Sangaya can be said to revolve around shift when a sudden change from hatred to love emerges between Maina and Zubaina compared to the previous scene when viewers see Maina kicking Zubaina, the maid. The situation suggests that people are bound to experience changes in their lives. It means that no condition is permanent. The symbol of hatred has metamorphosed to the emblem of love. If the societies can persist in continuing positive cultural changes in this manner, then every place will be heaven on earth and every person can be a potential friend. Apparently, in a long shot, viewers see the couple walking in a slow motion while soundtrack music plays. They eventually sing facing each other. Maina dresses in blue trousers, white long sleeve shirt, blue waist coat and a black cap to match, and sings a four minutes song with Zubaina, who dresses in Fulani attire of sleeveless *riga* and *zane* (blouse and a piece of cloth tied round the waist by a woman). All these are physical objects used in the video film to confirm her identity, as opposed to the abstract images in the folktale. The on-screen song performance does not only increase viewers' attention on the image, but it also changes their perception of conditions of life and reminds them that song and dance are totally integrated into and related to their daily existence. In rural areas particularly, song and dance continue to play an integral role in various domestic activities and social occasions.

Sabo pays attention to both action and narration in developing the plotlines of *Sangaya*. He combines different events including those that cause tension, especially those who intrude by following only their inclinations. Sabo calls for a change and rethinking of the self-centered attitude. Rather than self-reliance and egoism, people should consider other people's feelings. Anything short of this may escalate into resistance and crisis, as Kilishi challenges the heroine's intrusion of Zubaina. Despite the conjuncture of events, Sabo is able to link the sequences. The video film can be said to be linear in structure. His style tallies with what Phillips (2005:270) asserts. According to him, most makers of narrative films arrange scenes chronologically. While some film analysts might look at this development as a filmmaker's shortfall in technical know-how for presenting a broad spectrum of scenes, this study considers Sabo's *Sangaya* as a video film in which there is a shift. It involves incorporating an old medium into a new one and making the two media converge to form a mass media, as Kaschula (2001:xii) says, ""it pertains to our fast-changing society and scholars should guard against seeing it as inflexible"". The aim might be to revisit some cultural motifs, define the sequences at which they operated and then undergo some changes. For example, the relationship between Maina and Zubaina, to Sabo, should not be considered as a relationship that involves only two people. Therefore, viewers see Maina urging his friend to see Azumi (Zubaina), the girl of his choice. When they meet, in a close up shot, the camera captures only Maina and Zubaina cutting off his friend, Nura. When the three of them appear on screen in a long shot, viewers see Nuru talking to Azumi on behalf of Maina although in Maina''s presence. Being a prince, he does not need to talk too much as in real situations, sometimes king''s subject talks on his behalf. Azumi agrees to marry Maina on one condition, which she demands to know from his friend. She asks him this question: Can he marry me in any condition he sees me? (*Sangaya* 00:45:57 minutes). The question seems difficult to Nuru therefore he keeps quiet, gets back and allows Maina to move closer to talk for himself. He moves closer to Azumi and in a close up shot, the camera captures only Maina and Azumi, cutting off Nura, his friend. Cutting off Nura is another aspect that is in the foreground regarding the issue of change in this work. There is a shift from hatred, an outrageous theme on which the video film starts. Apparently, the film announces its emotional tone. It does not only cut off Nura, but it goes on to show only an actor and actress (the two protagonists) in a close-up shot to suggest the kind of switch in courtship comparable to traditional style in which Chamo (2012:60) states that ""'in the traditional practice, marriage is a serious matter of the family, but not of the couple'''. In a related dimension, what brings a further point of departure from a traditional form of courtship and injects change is Zubaina's failure to come along with her girlfriend or at least a young girl, whose presence serves as a check against any attempt that may tarnish the reputation of their families.

The film links back to contemporary Hausa society. In contemporary courtship, there is less emphasis on escort as a boy and girl can meet without much interference. The society has realized the need for people to come together and interact. More importantly, when intending couples come together freely, they will understand each other. When they eventually marry, the marriage will last. It will result into what is now commonly known as *mutu ka raba*, a phrase that means till death do us part. Although the issue of *auri saki* (persisted divorce) compared to *mutu ka raba* is not an issue in the video film, it remains a social problem in the society. There are many divorcees, whose marriages could not last because they do not go through intimate courtship free from the traditional interference from parents.

> Wato babban abin takaici shi ne kamar yadda mu Hausa-Fulani muke yakana da tsantsami wajen riko da addini, amma abin mamaki sai ki same mu mu ne kan gaba wajen yawaita auri-saki da tarin zaurawa da makamantansu. Wannan matsala ce babba. Ko me yake kawo irin wannan? (*Zaurawa* 00:51:46).

Translation

> In fact, the major element of indignation is how we, the Hausa-Fulani, claim to uphold religious values, but unfortunately we are foremost in divorce, which results in many divorcees. This is a big problem and I wonder what could be the cause of the problem?

Evidently, *auri saki* (persisted divorce) and *zaurawa* (divorcees) are two aspects of life that are not only problematic, but they have not been overcome yet. Halima Atete, an actress agrees with Buhari as her response to him was: "*Gaskiya ne, kusan gida daidai ne babu zaurawa*". (It is true there is a divorcee in almost every family) (*Zaurawa* 00:51:52)[13]

Logically, this is what *Sangaya* discourages and then introduces a change. When Zubaina asks Nura concerning Maina, he does not only give an answer to the question, but he also moves away from them so that he does not intervene in their discussion nor hear Maina''s response, which can be considered his personal affair. In addition, the director reiterates the change when he cuts off Nura from the discussion to signify that this is a welcome change. The traditional *auren dangi* in the society is experiencing a shift and *Sangaya* delves into this development. Although Maina and Kilishi marry as cousins, *Sangaya* video film does not give preference to this kind of marriage. Rather, it highlights a shift to a kind of marriage that is based on mutual understanding and not only based on family descent, lineage and pedigree. There is a shift from genealogy involving families (sometimes without the knowledge of their children) to

---

13 Al-amin Buhari and Halima Atete in a dialogue express their concern on the issue of divorce in the film *Zaurawa* (2013). The concern of Buhari and Atete is the representation of the concern of the government of Kano State when the government discovered that there are many broken homes due to divorce. To tackle this problem, the governor of Kano State, Rabi"u Musa Kwankwaso gave financial assistance to divorcees that were willing to get married.

mutuality involving each of two persons, a boy and a girl. To demonstrate the shift, the camera captures Zubaina receiving a ring from Maina. The ring does not only symbolize agreement to a relationship, but it also symbolizes commitment to a certain course by two persons, synonymous to the use of an engagement ring in contemporary marital relationships. Tradition encourages the idea of uniting a prince to a princess, a consideration of status especially among the aristocrats. Although Maina and Kilishi are united in marriage, the same *Sangaya* manifests a departure from this conservative idea and presents a change by showing Maina, the prince, marrying Zubaina, a maid.

Sangaya aims to present a bond that unites couples but the bond is not complete until intending couples seek the approval and blessing of parents. In some video films, from day one a boy meets a girl, viewers see on screen *bayan aure* (after wedding). But Sabo does not undermine the issue of involving parents in the institution of marriage. Rather, he places emphasis on it, as viewers see Zubaina's introduction to Maina''s mother. Although Zubaina initially takes another form, as in performance thereby attracting Maina, now she has gone back to her original form. This development is similar to the temporal aspect of performance in which performers are changed and later returned to their starting place. It is called transportation because of the change from one time or space reference to another. The technique of character transformation in films, which the film director employs leads to rejection. He transforms Zubaina back to herself, the wretched child Maina knows. His mother demands to know from Zubaina if she is the girl her son meets. Zubaina gives an affirmative response "I am the girl he meets and here is the ring he gives to me" (*Sangaya* 00:53:53 minutes). This answer follows with a detailed narration of how the romantic affair starts between her and Maina. However, Sabo departs from the type of narration which involves repetition. Rather, he uses flashback and this technique is another aspect of metamorphosis that this work considers. In folktale, the narrator takes all the roles in the storyline and acts in different manners, but typical of each character. The audience sees only the narrator. But in the video film, there is a massive shift regarding dual functions by the narrator. His role of narrator as actor(s) in which he has the monopoly is curtailed. There is a shift from activities by one man to activities by individuals. It can be right to say that the video film has given preference to the culture of division of labor in information dissemination in comparison with the tradition of monopoly of a narrator.

Reference to events that happened before that are important for the storyline require the narrator to repeat it. This kind of narration especially narration within a narration is shifted in the video film whereby previous events of the actors are shown in a series of flashbacks, a technique which is not used by the traditional storyteller. While Wynchank (1994:17) shows that prolepsis (flash forward) and analepsis (flashback) are modern techniques unknown to traditional practitioners of orality, Phillips (2005:66) explains with respect to flashback that "viewers see a brief scene, or (rarely) a sequence that interrupts a film narrative to show earlier events". It is a technique used by filmmakers in order to save time and energy. One example of flashback Sabo injects into the video film is a previous scene involving Maina and Zubaina. Rather than having Zubaina retell the event to the Queen, Sabo does the retelling through flashback. He does not only save Zubaina's energy, but he also saves time for the next dialogue. However, saving time is not decisive, but the fact that, for film viewers, action is much more interesting than lengthy dialogues. Immediately the flashback is cut off, viewers hear the Queen's remark of approval as she says, "It is the will of God for Maina and Zubaina to be a couple" (*Sangaya* 00:57:38 minutes). The Queen's approval and the film's emphasis on the marriage between Maina and Zubaina as well as between Maina and Kilishi reinforce *auren gata* and inject a sense of shift in status. It does not only depict the idea of moving from grass to grace, but it shows that the rich also cry. However, what is new is the degree of boldness and high level of sincerity by which Maina's mother (a Queen notwithstanding) tackles the situation in a society in which the concept of man-woman binarism is prominent. To borrow from Olusegun Adekoya's (2014:335) words, she comes from the society where the traditional gender hierarchy in which the male is the head and the female is his foot-mat. Her boldness is synonymous with taking the wrappings off the traditional *kunya* (shame) without necessarily considering the implications. Therefore, her decision (at the absence of her husband), as the video film shows, does not only showcase shift towards new trends and development, but it also indicates that a Hausa/Fulani woman is gradually coming of age, not in the sense of competing with men, but at least in participating in a crucial decision in the family. Indirectly, Maina's mother, on behalf of other women, strongly protests against the traditional practise of patriarchy in Hausa society. She exhibits a frankness and boldness which should serve as a demonstration for cultural change regarding rights of women. Since this metamorphosis does not happen in an empty space therefore, it becomes important for the filmmaker to react to the rising flexibility in his effort to record and reflect on the changing and challenging circumstance.

Kishi (rivalry) excels in Sabo's *Sangaya*, particularly between Zubaina and Kilishi. Even though in the beginning of the film Maina hates Zubaina, his hatred is not based on *kishi*. An example of a representation of a typical *kishi* is the attitudes of Kilishi towards Zubaina. A proverb in Hausa on *kishi* says, *kishi kumallon mata, in ya motsa sai ya fito*. It means that among women, rivalry is like a trigger and when it is pulled, it causes anger which leads to domestic crisis. To Kilishi, it is not the co-wife issue that is the most disturbing situation. To her, that is normal among Muslim Hausa. She knows that the society she belongs to is a polygamous society. Her family in particular is not an exception. Her agony is the rivalry from a servant who is now a fellow co-wife. She and her servants confirm the above proverb, *kishi kumallon mata, in ya motsa sai ya fito*, by despising, castigating and ridiculing Zubaina verbally,

Kilishi: Tashi ki ɗau tsintsiya ki share mini bayan ɗaki. Duɓe ta tana tafiya ƙugu a karkace. Yanzu fa sai wani namiji ya ce yana son ta ko?

Abokiya 1: Anya kuwa? Ai duk namijin da ya auri wannan ya yi asara kuma shi ya rako maza duniya

Abokiya 2: Ni kam ina namiji ka ba ni wannan da gida da dawakai bakwai, ba zan karɓe ta ba, sai in ce a kai kasuwa (*Sangaya* 00:42:05 minutes).

Tanslation

Kilishi: Get up, go and clean my toilet. Look at her walking, her back is bend. As she is, is there a man who wants to marry her?

Friend 1: I doubt it. Any man who wants to marry this "thing" makes a big mistake and he is just an escort to men into the world.

Friend 2: As for me, if I was a man and you give me this "thing" to marry along with seven horses, I will not take the offer. I will say take it to the market to another bidder (*Sangaya* 00:42:05 minutes).

The director shifts from narration to song and action. He changes the dialogue to a 5 minutes 30 seconds contest of self-expression in a song and dance involving Maina, Kilishi, Zubaina (Ali Nuhu, Hauwa Ali Dodo, Fati Muhammad) and other female dancers as extras (*Sangaya* 01:05:02 minutes). The song plays a prominent narrative role in which the camera focuses on the whole characters, highlighting its oneness. While the song entertains viewers and calm down tension in them, it also answers the question of diegetic because the soundtrack music the viewers hear is constructed as issuing from the storylines. Viewers hear the source of conflict between Kilishi and Zubaina in the song. The song's lyrics comment on the incidents in the film's main narrative and announce the events that will come to pass. Each character continues to ridicule her rival''s jealous attributes and then reintroduces the anticipated incident. On one hand, viewers hear Kilishi in an explicit and convincing voice stating her reasons why she feels Maina should marry her. She claims she is from a royal family like him. She is his first girlfriend and everyone knows they are engaged. On the other hand, Zubaina sings and counteracts Kilishi's somewhat unworkable legacy of royal upbringing by expressing why she deserves to be Maina's wife. She states how she suddenly rises up out of something which has been immersed or sunk and appears in sight. But these are not enough reasons for a man to maintain one wife, as it is common among Muslim Hausa men to marry a second, third or fourth wife the moment they feel they attain a relatively higher social status. Therefore, the self-expression unfolds a departure from the traditional system of courtship and marriage. Traditionally, a girl does not need to blow her own trumpet in order to attract suitors. One girl can have many suitors. But gone are the days when girls were scarce commodities. The number of unmarried young girls and spinsters is increasing on a daily basis. And as culture is dynamic, it is not surprising to see women dating young boys and providing their needs. Both personal and parental status of a girl is a necessary advantage for securing her a husband to suggest that now there is little or no emphasis on true love. Rather, it is unconditional and based on materialism.

Sangaya remains a remarkable and commercially ostentatious Kannywood video film, as its soundtrack music still thrills viewers. Its success is due to the song and choreographic dance the director employs. In the words of Adamu (2007:56-57), "*Sangaya* [...] captured the imagination of Hausa urban audience. The music, and most especially the choreography, from the sound track catapulted the video into the charts of "big league" Kannywood video films, and one of the most successful Kannywood films of all time". Thus, the use of choreography in the video film does not only signify metamorphosis, but it also makes a significant breakthrough in Kannywood industry. It is the first video film to inject musical hybridity through the combination of both traditional and modern (musical) instruments. It is another aspect of shift that highlights the striking contrast between the application of songs in folktale and video film such as *Sangaya*.

Sabo's film *Sangaya* creates a significance for his viewers. The way of the world in the film is regenerative and can itself be considered a filmic extension of the African oral tradition anchored by narrator, who combines song, dance and narratives in order to entertain viewers and to reinforce their collective identity. Therefore, a close look at *Sangaya* might reveal not only filmic creativity, but also the manifestation of metamorphosis in Hausa culture.

Ancient Practice Performance Video Film: *Borin Ibro (2008)*

Content of *Borin Ibro*

The video film's discussion centers on electoral malpractice, exploring the particular incidence when the candidate who wins the election is not the candidate who is sworn-in. Even though politics is not the main subject matter of the video film, it is a representation of a critical approach to politics which is based on fraud. It shows that elections are not always free and fair and leadership is more of an appointment rather than a democratic election. Although it is not mentioned in the video film, the need to embrace an acceptable type of orientation and a system of principles, especially in the contemporary political administration, is made clear.

In what follows after this political shot, the video film centers on spirit possession as already evident in *bori* cult. The director reiterates a belief in spirits on three different occasions, which I consider as the director''s device to put emphasis on his subject of attention, repetition being a classical rhetorical device to do so. Viewers see Ibro and Daushe, the two protagonists, leaving their village for another city, *yawon ci rani* (migration for temporary work), in search of "greener pastures". In addition to the desire for a better future, Joseph McIntyre uses terms such as social breakdown, social collapse and radical change or social transformations to describe what necessitates migration. According to him, for the Hausa, the original breakdown starts in their homeland or native country. Evidently, Ibro and Daushe encounter obstacles such as hunger and thirst on the way. These obstacles come to an end when they meet an old man, played by Baba Ari, fetching water from a well in the first village in which they arrive. But they become worried and the viewers can see the anger and frustration in their facial expression when they ask for water to drink but the old man refuses to give any to them. They assume he is a spirit and their assumptions prepare the minds of the viewers to what the filmmaker wants to communicate. Hausa viewers are likely to see a representation of a common belief among some communities, namely that old people are associated with spirits. When Ibro and Daushe go farther, they meet a woman by a well again and ask her for water. At the beginning she refuses to talk and that makes them to form a common consent on the people of the village about spirit possession. They emphasize their perception of the village along the villagers and on hearing their comment, the woman breaks her silence to emphasize their perception. Consequently, her statement does not only confirm the two protagonists'' assumption, but it also motivates them to see the need to embark on *bori* in order to rid the village of spirits.

While some filmmakers present what the plotlines aim to represent at the beginning of their video films, Auwal Y. Abdullahi's *Borin Ibro* shows a departure from this technique by with-holding information. However, the technique gives viewers an advantage by affording them the chance to watch varieties of information. When the information that is withheld is revealed in a later scene, it becomes what Phillips (2005:271) refers to as "privileged placement". From the onset, viewers hear dialogues on politics. The discussions on politics, which the filmmaker employed in the video film is a device to make viewers see the kind of politics, which develops on malpractice, and if Nigeria needs to develop, at least politically, then Nigerians must collectively embrace a progressive change in their political thoughts. Beside this intruding start, the plot of the video film is marked by cases of shifts from the traditional to the modern in sequence. At the palace of the village head, while he sits on a bench, his courtiers sit on a mat to signify leader and subject relationship in traditional set-ups. However, the camera brings out a glaring juxtaposition about modern belief system and traditional belief system to suggest that this attitude may be a rational in uncovering that presently, the Hausa can go to *bori* cult for cures without necessarily being members of the cult or worshiping the spirits above Allah. In a close-up shot, viewers see Ari's right hand counting the beads in his rosary and as the camera moves slowly for a long shot, he is seen chanting incantations silently while an off-screen music is playing. Viewers see how the director brings the two belief systems together to emphasize the difference between them and to exemplify a shift from pre-Islamic to Islamic belief system. This development suggests the continuous changing pattern in Hausa societies in particular and Nigeria in general. Kofoworola and Lateef (1987:2) observe that ancient religious beliefs and practices could be identified in some aspects of such customs, but the modern Islamic believers (of course Christianity too) will deride those contemptuously as superstitious beliefs and practices.

On the account of tradition, people express their agonies and Ibro and Daushe assume that the village head and his courtiers are bereaved by their facial expressions. They are silent and are looking moody as well. Contrary to their expectation, the princess is not dead, but suffering from *ciwon aljannu* (sickness caused by the spirit). The video film does not heighten the intensity of the characters'' antagonism, but showcases their ambivalence, points of convergence and mixed feelings about spirit possession in contemporary time. On one hand, Ibro and Daushe are of the opinion that the villagers are spirits. On the other hand, the courtiers are suspecting Ibro and Daushe for the occurring misfortunes in the village since their arrival. They may not be spirits, but by implication, they can cause havoc and miseries in the society. In this development, the video film is marked by a shift from the traditional belief that only the spirits are associated with misfortunes. However, Ibro and Daushe are able to cure the princess through jokes and not by *bori* procession. Their action signifies the impact of humor. It does not only suggest a shift from believing that every sickness is caused by spirits, but it also indicates that it is not only by invoking spirits that a sick person can become cured. The video film implies that negligence can cause nervous tension, as seen from the princess when she is forsaken by her family. Ironically, the village head and his courtiers are happy about Ibro and Daushe's curative powers.

They believe that the protagonists can cure, not necessarily by supernatural powers.

Transformation of *bori* in the Film *Borin Ibro*

A reflection on *bori* performance will reveal the traditional pattern and involvement in the search for the solutions to curative problems and forms of disorderliness. Although this is what the video film represents, this work explores some changes that are encountered in the making. In this regard, the work considers that *Borin Ibro* as a video film is not only about entertainment, but it is also an avenue for promoting and preserving traditional elements in a new medium. The dance, sound tracks and demonstrations, which viewers witness in the video film, are often replicated initiation ceremonies in arena when a character is seeking for a particular favor from supernatural powers. The shift of action from arena to video film more often than not is either an overstatement or a reduction of actions. In *Borin Ibro*, viewers do not only see the reduction of the traditional elements, but they also see only portrayals, which the film depicts through the characters and it can be described as a cinematic appropriation of *bori* cult. The film does not replenish *bori* again, but it echoes the past and explores outstanding prowess for controlling the supernatural in a new manner. In this regard, what used to be a performance involving audience during events like naming and wedding has become an event without live audience in the video film. It could be a result of the director''s attempt to save costs. Neither does he engage the services of extras to act as audience nor resort to footage of crowds in a different event. As a result, the scene looks unnatural and depicts an example of transformation, which reduces the richness of the performance. Also, among the traditional instruments employed during *bori* performance like *garaya* (stringed pluked lute), *goge* (one stringed bowed lute) and *kwarya* (large gourd), only *buta* (small gourd-rattle) is employed in the video film, marking a shortage in the application of varieties of instrumental music. This development contributes to the decline of the required objective representation of *bori* as performance.

Furthermore, during *bori* performance, usually four categories of principal actors are present. There are musicians who supply music and display their skills, spectators who come purposely for entertainment, those who are possessed with spirits and require cure and those who perform the ritual curing. The presence of spectators signifies that though *bori* can be regarded as a cult, it is not performed in a secret place or shrine. The spectators are not only entertained by the musical performance, but also by those who are possessed with spirits when they are displaying their repertoires. In *Borin Ibro,* only two categories of people are seen: the curer and possessed person. While Ibro plays the role of curer, Ari plays the character of a possessed person. This development signifies that the performance in the video film is characterized by changes. This does not only concern the absence of spectators, but it is also associated with the non-availability of musicians that form part of the major participants at the event of *bori*.

Borin Ibro as a video film on *bori* performance has another remarkable change from the perspective of space. Considering performance space, as Schechner (1988:14) explains, unlike office or home, performance space is used on an occasional rather than steady base. During performance, large parts of the day and often for days on end, spectators get pleasure from being entertained. Traditionally, whenever a performance starts, the space is utilized intensely, attracting large number of spectators who come for the scheduled event. In respect of preparation, the space is uniquely organized so that a large group of spectators can watch a small group and the event gives the feelings of ceremony and celebration that promote social solidarity. *Borin Ibro* is not only marked by the non-availability of a befitting space, it is characterized by lack of spectators at shooting. This is not unconnected to the issue of cultural change. Since culture is dynamic, the practice of *bori* is affected by the dynamism of culture. Therefore, *bori* is not only seen as extinct culture, but it is also not popular in the society now.

The act or display of curative powers is one important activity of *yan bori* (bori adherents) and viewers see two representations of this activity in the video film *Borin Ibro*. In respect of acting, this is one key area where the camera is used to show the trends of events. The camera is directed by the cameraman, who is directed by the film director in a very conscious way. Therefore, viewers see that most of the actions are framed in close-up shots where they note moods of anger, fear, frustration, tension and determination. When Ibro is performing the ritual of curing on Ari, the person who is alleged to have been possessed with spirit is marked by jokes, less tension and determination compared to the traditional *bori* that was characterized with all the seriousness it deserved.

During the process of curing, in a close-up shot viewers see Ari making fun of the situation by creating jokes as he struggles to get up, giving more emphasis on the entertainment aspect than the curative dimension. This development creates a setback in Ibro's determination to set Ari free from the spirits that possessed him. It is part of a major change in today's approach to *bori*. Not even the arrival of Ɗangwari from another village for curative aspect can recapture *bori* and saturate the place with it. Rather, his arrival explores the factor that influences the manner spirit possession is changed and announced.

> Na zo neman lafiyana ne. Aljannu ne suna damuna. Muna da aljannu na gidanmu, na babanmu ɗaya ne. To, sai an sami wani, amma an ce na yi wani baƙon aljannu kuma baƙin aljannu ne. Shi ne na ji an ce mani idan na zo nan garin na yi tambaya, akwai wanda na yi aikin aljannu na bori. Shi ne nake so a yi mini taimako a cire mini wannan aljannu. (*Borin Ibro* 00:35:36 minutes).

Translation

> I come for my health. The spirits are troubling me. We have the spirit of our family (deity). Our father has one spirit, but later there is an additional one. I was told I have a strange spirit and it is the wicked type. Therefore, I was directed to come to this village because someone is casting out spirits and I would like him to cast them out of me. (*Borin Ibro* 00:35:36 minutes)

Although there is music to invoke the spirits, Ɗangwari feigns an emotion. He pretends to have been possessed and he is not sure if to announce the arrival of the spirits to him or their departure from him. Uncertainty is a case of change that is influenced by lack of commitment, as Ɗangwari is only seen feigning the character that goes from the ordinary world to the performing world. His aspect of *bori* is not performed with great enthusiasm for a cultural heritage. Traditionally, he is to set about his task of battling the spirits with vigor, if not for cultural heritage, at least for his health. But he is seen doing things which he can do ordinarily without being fully transported. The work of the transported is to enter the performance, play his role, which is usually acting as the agent for larger forces, or possessed directly by them. Subsequently, viewers assume that no type of behavior exists separately from Ɗangwari.

It means that *bori* is now characterized with less or no transmission, manipulation and transformation of behavior, while performers should exhibit some signs such as recovery, remembrance or even invent behavior. On one hand the video film as a medium transforms *bori* into a weak performance. On the other hand, the video film represents what is actually going on in the society about *bori*. Since it is becoming extinct, it has no longer a stronger medial capacity. Therefore, the distorted form becomes convincing in the film's plot. Evidently, the film could be used just as a reference material to *bori* because as the analysis indicates, the performance is in decline.

Analysis of *Tashe* (2010)

Content of *Tashe*

The video film *Tashe* is about a classical Hausa performance tradition known as *tashe*. The film starts with a scene featuring Hauwa Garba, a performer who goes into a couple''s room. However, she will not carry out the performance, as the couple drives her away because she enters the room without excuse. Like Hauwa, Daushe and Gatari, two other characters decide to organize *tashe*. They become motivated after watching *tashe* performance by Ali Nuhu and Adam A. Zango. Daushe and Gatari resolve to perform *Tashi Wali* (The Saint Will Fly). They plan for a rehearsal because it is important in performance, as freelance singers also rehearse. Besides rehearsal, Daushe and Gatari discuss the performance material they require such as costume, which is another prominent item in performance. During rehearsal, which includes additional performers such as Ari, 'Dan''auta and Tukur, Ari, an old man plays the role of *gwauro*. The scene gives a glimpse of the *tashe* known as *gwauro tashi gari ya waye* (get up it is dawn), which is performed to mock a bachelor. Garba S. K, who plays the role of the king comes across the performers and gives them some money. As justice is not done in sharing the money, disagreement becomes the preeminent characteristic of the group. Daushe who claims to be leader takes the biggest share of the money, which makes the group split into two and each group goes to perform *tashe*. However, the *tashe* turns out to be unpleasant, as three people report the bitter experiences they encounter from the two groups of the *tashe* performers.

Tashe and its Contemporary Transformations in the Video Film

As an old tradition, the main aim of *tashe* is to amuse people in the month of Ramadan when Muslims observe fasting. Instead of depicting the traditional format, the video film turns out to show a unique and urbanized way of performance - some more recent shifts from the traditional. In contrast, the villagers around the performers of *tashe* are likely to be part of a closely knit community. On the contrary, in the cinema or viewing center as the case may be, the viewers sitting row by row, facing the screen, watching *tashe* video film, more often than not have no sense of belonging to a group, as a viewer might not know the next person sitting beside him.

One major change takes place when performers perform beyond the limited period of *tashe.* This development uncovers the influence of popular culture and globalization on local culture. The narrative allows viewers to critically explore the traditional and the post-Islamic time. One way of analyzing *tashe* is to look at transformative forces at work through the point of view from which a video film is created and received. A film narrative can be understood from at least two perspectives. On the one hand: What is the particular way of thinking of the filmmaker when it comes to his perspective - how does he/she create situations in the film? On the other hand, the position from which viewers see actions in the film enables them to see the world in a specific manner and time. Regarding *Tashe,* from the viewpoint of viewers, at first glance the video film operates within the perspective of conventional performance that affords them to see a mimetic reproduction of a particular recreational performance. But from the perspective of the film's director, there is a change in the status quo involving culture and custom, which is visible in the film. Basically, the manner in which the culture operates is different from how it appears in the video film.

From the choice of location, particularly market, the video film can best be explained from the point of view of the contemporary. The choice of market as location therefore indicates a shift in the performance from the traditional, which begins after breaking the fast to the one, which begins even at the point of fasting. This shift is made possible within a broader shift in material gains, as there is a large audience in the market engaged in selling their wares to earn profit; performers stand at high chance of getting a little part of traders' gain compared to when they move from house to house in the traditional way.

The traditional sense of humor in *tashe* performance shifts to humiliation in the video film. As a performance for pleasure, it is meant to make people pass time pleasantly. But the video film shows that nowadays some performers misuse *tashe's* humorous intention to humiliate, insult and offend people through rude remarks for not getting a present for the performance they have undertaken. This development indicates that there is a shift from emphasis on entertainment to emphasis on financial gains. It might be as a result of the shift from contentment with the little to an excessive demand for more. We are now living in a competitive world where people are after wealth acquisition by all means. There is a change in the economic status of the citizenry where public funding is not circulating as it is supposed to be because only few individuals are in control. Although viewers can get amused from the songs in the video film, it is obvious in the film plot that some of those to whom *tashe* is performed are not happy because they are greeted with rude remarks. Giving negative comments to the audience does not only annoy them, but it also shows how the event is changing at a time when peace of mind is required rather than tension. In principle *tashe* was traditionally performed by young people. But nowadays they seldom perform it. The effect of this is mediated by video film, which showcases some changes.

The traditionally allocated space for *tashe* is the *kofar gida* (compound's frontage terrace), but in the film *Tashe* under review, the director presents Hauwa in the beginning of the video film, as she enters the room of a couple and says she comes to perform for them. Viewers see her entering the room in an unusual manner, hence it is very strange. She does not care to say *salamu alaikum*, the usual greeting on arrival at someone's domain or at least the corrupted Hausa version, *sallama dai.* She moves in speedily in order to avoid being stopped. It is a device that the director employs to indicate that the message is not complete until she enters the room to suggest that in today's *tashe* performance, the status quo is violated. As a result of this violation, people do not get amused; therefore they have no much interest in it any more. They have fear that those who undermine the tradition of *tashe* will ridicule them. This is an evidence to support the claim that it is not only Kannywood video films that enhance the breach of culture. The work through the video film *tashe* does not only show that there are other sources but, it also suggests that the custodians of culture play the primary role in determining the course of their culture.

Traditionally, *tashe* performers perform whether they are given gifts or not. The audience is entertained and the performers will come again the next day. But the situation is no longer the same these days. When performers approach the audience for *tashe*, instead of watching it, they avoid the performers by going inside the compound. Based on this, one can say that there is a shift in *tashe* because some unpatriotic and undesirable people are changing the manner in which it should be performed. The video film serves as a mirror into the dynamism of culture. The cultural change is evident through the principles and practices by those undesirable performers and their provocative and ill-mannered remarks. The way the director uses the character of Hauwa through her costume and action particularly when she says she has come to perform *tashe* in the beginning of the video film shows the director's device in calling the attention of viewers to a new pattern of performance. Thus, the starting plotlines help in showing how the video film rises up out of something that has been there already and how it reveals a departure from its classical form. In a way, now *tashe* has come out and is cropping up to become an event which is influenced by the youths.

Through the character of Ari who asks Hauwa if *tashe* is supposed to be performed in the room when she meets him in the room, the video film uncovers the kind of shift from the traditional to modern, particularly from the point of view of Ari who plays the role of an old man. On the part of Hauwa, as a young woman, she could not separate performance space from social space. Viewers see Hauwa realizing that she encroaches upon Ari's domain and by implication his privacy by her new form of *tashe* which differs from conventional one. Thus, the director employs what can be considered the conventional wisdom when he uses the character of Daushe and Gatari to showcase various types of *tashe* at close shot in comparison to Hauwa's *tashe* thereby exploring a change from the traditional to modern especially when Daushe and Gatari plan for a rehearsal. This development does not only emphasize the effect of rehearsal in contemporary performance, but it also depicts the influence of global music in traditional performance especially when they only mention popular musicians such as Michael Jackson and Billy O and then stress that they undergo rehearsal before they perform. It is pertinent to mention that *Tashe* depicts change from behavioral norm of honesty and trust to uncultural and uncompromising behavior of dishonesty and distrust. This example of shift is seen in the video film when performers are sharing the gifts they get. They do not show justice in sharing, as such there is turmoil and disagreement among them. Daushe who proves to be the leader takes the greater share of the gifts. Evidently, his action is a depiction of the idiomatic expression, *kashin dankali* (pile of potatoes) which is synonymous to the manner big potatoes are placed on top of small ones. When one relates this representation to the development in contemporary Hausa society, it entails that in today's *tashe* the least privileged are deprived of a certain freedom because *kashin dankali* basically includes the meaning 'to cheat'. It is a representation of how some people, particularly the bourgeoisie, are oppressing the masses, especially when the full idiomatic expression, *kashin dankali babba mai danne kanana* (pile of potatoes in which the big ones press the small ones) is taken into consideration. It might be right to say that in today's *Tashe*, the participants exhibit a departure from contentment to greed, as demonstrated by 'Dan'auta and Tukur in *Mai Kwadayi Tashi Mana* (Hey you, Mr Glutton, get away) in the film. This performance in this film discredits those kids who become voracious on seeing food and will not like to go until they are given. In principle, it is not only indicating a moral shift, but also suggesting a message aimed at advising people against greed.

Decline in standards of morality and behavior, otherwise known as moral decadence, are manifest in *Tashe* to symbolize shift. Basically, the month of Ramadan is a holy month therefore people should remain holy and also fast. But the video film shows a group of performers who depart from the modus operandi. They do not only confiscate food from a boy, but they also eat it within fasting hours. Abdullahi Baba Lado is a victim of moral decadence in *Tashe* as he encounters public embarrassment through the performers' comments. Rather than to employ the services of film's extras, the director shoots the video film in a normal location where there are normal day's activities. In such location, what is likely to affect the smooth flow of storylines of the video film is the ambient sound from the movement of the public, vehicles or their horns. But, the director has successfully cleared away the background noise hence viewers do not experience any sound that can distract them from hearing the video film's discourses and seeing Lado's disgusting situation. They are able to notice the emergence of a new *tashe* in which they are potential culprits and subjects of ridicule if they fail to offer performers some gifts.

From the point of view of change in *tashe* from performance to video film, another evident difference between the two, apart from the change affected by technological innovations, is that of verbal expression. In traditional oral performance, the audience saw performers focusing on checking and balancing cultural norms. Their roles were based more on moralizing. In the video film, the lens is focused on the performers, whose interest is to ridicule others and to amass wealth by collecting gifts. In the process, there is a shift away from entertainment and amusement which *tashe* had set for itself. The issue of cultural restrictions in areas considered to be morally offensive is dropped for personal aggrandizement. It may be right to say that some contemporary youths who partake in *tashe* are morally decadent because the video film shows that they manifest delinquent behaviors. In spite of the distinction between filmic representation and a general reality in society, the video film reflects on the behavior of some youths. In the video film, moral decadence is perceived in the society as an insignia of the youths. It is further foregrounded through the characters of Dan'auta, Tukur, Daushe, Gatari and Hauwa with their inappropriate attitudes. Hauwa's *tashe* is marked by a change in the starting day, which can be considered as a violation of rites. She starts on the fifth day while tradition demands that *tashe* begins on the tenth day of Ramadan. Dan'auta's variety of *tashe* is associated with a shift from mere posing a threat to a real hit-and-run syndrome. He does not only maintain the joking aspect of the performance, but he also knocks down a man and runs away. Traditionally, in this *tashe* known as *Zan Buge* (I Will Hit), the lead vocalist makes only one attempt to hit an audience present while the chorister restricts him by pulling him back as follows:

Waƙa: Zan buge

Amshi: Kar ka buge

Song: I will hit

Chorus: Do not hit

Daushe's sample of *Macukule* showcases a shift from emphasis on mutual co-existence to promotion of provocative statements among different ethnic groups, particularly Hausa and Gwari. More often than not, a *tashe* like *macukule* in a traditional dispensation is not meant to despise or to depict a contemptuous portrayal of an ethnic group particularly the Gwari, rather it is aimed at showing intercultural[14] joviality. But Daushe does not only change some terminologies in the video film by use of negative adjectives such as *marowaci, mayaudari* (miser, deceiver), but he also uses abusive language such as *idonsa kamar na barewa* (his face is like that of a gazelle) and *kunnuwansa kamar faranti* (his ears are like trays) to refer to a character in the presence of his girlfriend.

On a different level, change relates to a receiver behavioral shift with regard to the intra-diegetic gaze as contained in contemporary *tashe*. The concept of gaze in video film is characterized by who is viewing the film in general. The other dimension of gaze in particular involves the intra-diegetic gaze (Animasaun, 2011:40), which concerns a character gazing upon another character inside the film. Therefore, the analysis of the intra-diegetic gaze considers how a character looks at other character(s) with admiration or contempt and reflects upon what the character sees, whether or not the character adopts changes. As Animasaun (2011:43) puts it, the society has nevertheless remained increasingly integrated, but also highly differentiated as each group is reacting to its immediate environment in relation to the larger community. *Tashe* performance as an act of communication requires a sender, a receiver, a medium, a message and humor because a significant amount of human communication deals with humor. Therefore, humor influences viewers and persuades them to accept or reject what they see and hear. While it gives pleasure, creates playful moods, increases feelings of social solidarity and relieves tension, its transformation is based on the behavior of receivers' in *Tashe* video film. The senders ridicule the receivers and portray them as possessing negative attributes. For example, Daushe, a performer as sender ridicules Lado as receiver. As a performer sender, he ridicules Tukur, a performer as receiver in front of his girlfriend. The messages are based on pejorative stereotypes of the receivers' for example

---

14 In multi-ethnic Nigeria, there exist inter-ethnic jokes. One example is the joke between the Hausa and the Gwari. Although the jokes might sound contemptuous, the persons involved are not angry because they know it is meant to create humor.

one receiver is addressed as miser, deceiver, stingy, a verbal message in addition to gaze. Therefore, the resulting verbal assaults as well as the receiver's cultural values and expectations concerning appropriate social situation have affected cultural norms of politeness. As a result, through the additional verbal message, three people complain about the ridicule and embarrassment they receive from *tashe* performers.

One of the complainants reports that Daushe and Gatari's *tashe* differs from the traditional *tashe* because they meet him clearing his corn and they throw it on him and ridicule him at the same time. This is not how it is done, he emphasizes. For this complainant, *tashe* performance is allowed in Hausa culture, and it has been in practice during the month of Ramadan. Also it is a seasonal event, thus by implication it fulfills one of the situation markers in performance which is occasional principles. But the manner in which it is practiced in the video film is marked by changes. Another complainant reports that he is also a victim of change because performers throw his peacock into the well. As for a third complainant, performers meet him at his girlfriend''s house and they keep teasing him. While the reactions of the three receivers show a clear breach of the rules of standard social values, particularly peaceful co-existence, the response they receive from the village head uncovers the type of conventional *tashe* he knew. It is the type that the audience offer presents voluntarily and not under compulsion. In addition, a receiver's verbal reaction that, this is not how *tashe* is performed when he watches *Jatau Mai Magani* (Jatau the Medicine Man) is another clear example of shift: here it involves materials such as maize, photo album and radio instead of herbs used in the traditional performance. However, the situation shows a basic aspect of performance as the actual execution of an action in performance is never precisely a carbon copy of the other. Although some changes are encountered, the society is not silent about them. The director uses the character of an old man played by Baba Ari to warn Hauwa and his daughter, Ladidi, who are set to go out to perform *tashe* and by extension other girls who intend to perform it, not to go into a bachelor's house and to come back home early. Through Ari's profound warning, viewers hear how *tashe* is a tradition and how it has been in practice. In addition, the filmmaker presents an interlude of some *tashe* performance songs which may serve to boost cultural memory. However, those who know *tashe* performance in the arena could notice the changes and modifications from the *tashe* in the video film to suggest cultural shift.

Performative Action Video Film: *Fulani* (2012)

Content of *Fulani* (2012)

Fulani (2012) serves as an example of intertextuality in film, as *sharo* the element of reenactment of performance under review is more or less embedded in the plotlines of the film, *Fulani* (2012). The video film starts with Karima (played by Hadiza Mohammed) narrating to her son Kamal (played by Adam A Zango) about the bravery of the Fulani: how they live in the midst of wild animals in the bush and as nomads. According to her, Kamal will acknowledge them as outstanding brave people when he sees them at the point of *sharo*[15] performance. But Kamal gives a reluctant response to her, which is a sign of his disregard for tradition, as he does not know the performance and how it is practiced. As a youth who lives in the city, he has no knowledge of this custom. Incidentally, his mother tells him that he is also Fulani by lineage because his great grandparents are Fulani. However, his grandfather migrated to the city and lives there. This revelation motivates Kamal to move to the countryside, an entirely new environment and new culture for him. Gradually, he does not only acquaint himself with the people, but he also faces a challenge, which pushes him to participate in *sharo*, the common performance in the new

---

15 *Sharo* is a performance of flogging with a whip, during which the person being flogged is not expected to cry or show any sign of feeling pain. It is through this performance that a youth can prove to his parents and relatives that he can bear not only hardship, but can also take responsibility of being the head of a household. The performance originates as a result of dispute between two slaves. To settle the discord, the master of the slaves gave each of the two slaves a stick and requested them to beat one another in sequence, in order to see who is more brave by having the ability to put up with the strikes. There are two types of sharo performance: small and big. The small sharo is performed on occasions of ceremonies such as coronation, wedding and naming. It does not take a long time preparation and execution. The big sharo takes a longer time. It is performed between youths of different clans. Before it starts, a youth in clan A sends an arm band to another youth (his age-mate) in clan B, challenging him for a duel. Thus, the arm band is a symbol of challenge. The appropriate periods for this performance are: during harvest, when there is sufficient food for people and pastures for cattle to graze; and during cold season, as they believe that cold weather enhances healing of wounds, sustained from flogging. For more details, see Ahmed, Yahaya Mohammed. "A Preliminary Study of Soro Among the Fulbe of Yale" in *Harsunan Nijeriya.* ed. Daudu, Garba Kawu, Vol. XXII Kano: CSNL, BUK. 2010, 85-93 . use short form as always

environment. Against the wish of Malle and her family, Kamal challenges Magaji played by Zahradeen Sani in *sharo* and eventually wins to signal a new development of his cultural consciousness and personality. Therefore, the video film shows one example of a performance in a rural Hausa-Fulani community that dates back to the pre-colonial era. Perseverance in spite of opposition and difficulty recur in the video film, as Kamal experiences a new lifestyle, which includes a test of endurance.

Elements of Shift and Hybrid cultural Dimension in *Fulani* (2012)

The video film *Fulani* focuses on *sharo*, a traditional Fulani form of performance. The story copes with the changes in Hausa-Fulani society characterized by competing forms of entertainment such as the arena and the video film. This work does not only examine the use of performance in video film, but also the use of film in the reconstruction of a people's performance tradition. Indeed, *Fulani* contains alterations of the original performance because the filmmaker creates situations that have not existed in the tradition. By inference, in terms of shift, the video film can stylistically be a regeneration, as *sharo* is initially hidden or not immediately obvious although a traditional feature such as *tatsar nono*[16] is retained. In such a video film, considered as epic film, as Ayakoroma (2014:120) describes, "legends are transferred into our lifetime, in the sense that such production brings images of past heroes or communities back". However, it does not mean that *Fulani* (2012) is a duplicate of *sharo* because there are deeply embedded stories, which include turning points and inciting incidents for the purpose of maximum effect. This device of mixing sources according to Ayakoroma (2014: 122), could be responsible for the formulaic approach or stereotypical nature of many films. The filmmaker retains *sharo*'s traditional features and at the same time allows it to adapt to new qualities of the present time. According to Ayakoroma (2014: 124), the aim of incorporating new qualities by a filmmaker is to eulogize and stamp a notion about the valor and strength of the community to the viewer. I find Ayakoroma's assertion relevant to *Fulani*, as the filmmaker uses the role of Hadiza to highlight the bravery of the Fulani people for Kamal and by extension for the viewers. This is

---

16 These two episodes, performance and milking the cow are manifestation of the traditional life style, as the Fulani are known for this performance and are also known for rearing cattle.

an example of an outstanding change, as the performance of *sharo* does not feature or require any explanation because it is self-explanatory. The video film departs from the performance in its ability to express more dynamics of everyday existence and experience. And it does this, to borrow Adeshina Afolayan (2014:11) words, "through the privilege that films have as the dominant popular cultural form for packaging and repackaging everyday subjectivity". Being a fiction video film, *Fulani's* case of shift as its important quality lies in the flexibility based on the freedom to change the form and purpose of the performance. Therefore, the filmmaker uses the freedom available to him based on his point of view to express a new interpretation of an "old performance form" through a new process.

The video film depicts a change in ethnic merger and places emphasis on cultural and linguistic awakening. By inference, unlike the performance, the video film shows an outstanding ethnic merger between two ethnic groups that gives rise to the coinage Hausa-Fulani as an adopted linguistic entity. In a related sense, the video film showcases that two languages that are not only distinct, but are also from different linguistic phylum can merge. Furniss (1996:65) discusses how the Hausa and the Fulani have been living together for a long time and their ability to coexist has resulted into not only understanding, but also consent between them. While Hausa belongs to the Chadic group of languages, Fulfulde is in the Niger-Congo group along with Igbo and Yoruba, two of the three major languages in Nigeria. This development suggests that mutual coexistence in Nigeria requires tolerance when the linguistic and cultural complexities are considered. There is a portrayal of new life style that necessarily requires people to not only think about who they are, but also what they can do, at least in the context of contemporary Nigeria. Since the Fulani largely adopted Hausa as a second language, it is evident that they speak a hybrid Fulfulde.

The desire to have knowledge of a cultural event in his ethnic community and to participate in it makes Kamal to migrate to the rural area without considering what is said about rural areas. According to (Animasaun, 2011:48), "in most Nigerian movies the rural setting is depicted as dangerous". Based on this, most people migrate to the city, which is considered as a haven for greener pastures. *Fulani* operates a reversal of this kind of journey motif from the village to the city. Kamal relocates to the village without considering if something unpleasant is going to happen to him. He does not consider the predicament of unemployment and decadence symbolized by the witches, as one of the characteristics of the rural areas. Viewers see the transformation of Kamal, the son of a widow from what can be considered a modern family of three. By inference, the rural setting which Kamal migrates to needs to be developed so that indigenous knowledge and what it can offer can be accessed.

In his analysis of a Yoruba movie, *Ikekun Ola* (the door of wealth), Animasaun (2011:169) shows that the rural setting is communal contrary to the individualistic rural area. In the same vein through the journey of his protagonist Kamal, Yari depicts a change of mind-set in the journey motif and pays attention to the root by stressing more positive aspects of the rural settings. The video film is characterized by this journey motif: Kamal encounters some challenges before accomplishing a major task. In addition, there is also a structural relation to folktales in this motif. This technique which the director adapts creates a major shift, as the video film is seen to contain more narrative instead of action, which features prominently in the traditional performance of *sharo*. This study considers the journey motif as a social reality and the structuring device which is not visual during performance. What is of interest to the audience is the event, as it is the major action they come to watch. Therefore, journey motif to the performance by the performers is secondary to the audience. More often than not, they may or may not even notice it. As Thackway (2003:84) asserts, journeys often provide the central motor to events in the narrative and symbolize some form of initiatory quest for knowledge and wisdom, or battle between good and evil. It means that, in terms of structure, the video film is non-linear thus making a shift from the linear path to the end of the traditional *sharo* performance.

The filmmaker introduces a new life style to an undergraduate young man and by implication to the viewers. By virtue of his exposure, Kamal thinks he knows a lot, but he is surprised when he hears something new from his mother. The ethnic hybridity revealed in *Fulani* symbolizes a departure from the concept of Kannywood's characters being rooted in a specific ethnic formation. It suggests a manifestation of a possible cross-ethnic trajectory. As Tsika (2015:14) asserts, cross-ethnicity tends to nourish notions of good acting. Cross-ethnicity suggests cultural mixing and when people from different cultural backgrounds are brought together, they are easily integrated into the society, particularly a multi-lingual and multi-cultural country such as Nigeria. Kamal does not doubt the new ethnic specificity and affiliation, which his mother assigned to him, as she says to him *kai ma Fulani ne* (you are also Fulani) (*Fulani* 2012). More importantly, the scene shows change in the hidden cross-ethnic coexistence in contemporary time, to the point of regarding the diversity of Nigeria. Evidently, the video film showcases a shift from the notion of mono-ethnic industry to include a variety of ethno-linguistic groups that represent the different ethnic strands in northern Nigeria, similar to how Tsika (2015:15) describes Nigerian film's characters – they do not necessarily need to be kept or tied into one single knot. It may be right to say that even though Kannywood video films bear ethnic specificity or particularity, *Fulani* in particular departs from this claim to constitute a concrete aesthetics of cross-ethnic identity. For the Hausa characters in *Fulani,* the roles they take are not restricted to their ethnicity. They can not only be restricted to their culture, but they can also change to another culture easily and quickly in the manner they want in what Tsika (2015:17) describes as responsive to radical transformation.

The role of Zainab, a supporting actress, is used to expound the shift and to raise new cultural awareness. Zainab's role symbolizes a clarion call, a strongly expressed demand or request for action aiming at viewers to know where they come from: to consider their roots and who they are. The relevance of this call is that these days there are turbulent situations, particularly cases of ethnic clashes in northern Nigeria, especially in Plateau and Taraba states. In some localities, some ethnic groups claim they are the original natives while other ethnic groups are regarded as settlers. Primarily, Zainab injects change in people's mind-set and awakens them to tolerate other people by appreciating their cultures.

The video film represents *sharo* quite closely, with some changes. The changeover between city life and village life by Kamal changes both his attitude to life and the glamour of *sharo* when he participates in it as a non-professional. Viewers see him shift from a nuclear family that also changes to a single parent family after the demise of his father, and then to an extended family when he relocates to the rural area. There is evidently some irony in these shifting settings, because with the emergence of capitalism and the more recent structural adjustment policies and inflation in Africa, the nuclear family, as in developed countries becomes a financially viable social group, at least when Kamal's life in the city is compared to his life in the village.

The video film''s actions take place in both the city and the village, and focus on a relatively minor incident of changing base. Kamal insists on changing base because he knows where he is living, but he does not know where his parents come from. Like late Bob Marley says, "Going to our fatherland" in his album *Exodus* (1977), which expresses the eternal quest for land, identity and harmony, so is Kamal's case. When his mother says to him that he is also Fulani, who live in rural settlements, he feels motivated to go back to the roots. He is also going to see where his great grand parents lived. Gradually, this seemingly insignificant incident of changing base matures into *sharo* performance: a clash of two individuals involving Kamal of the city and Magaji of the village. The addition of the earlier scene in the city showcases the kind of change witnessed in *sharo*. However, the scene allows actions in the video film to get into the heart of the changes quickly and to move rapidly towards a conflict. The main conflict arises from the personalities of Magaji and Kamal, who represent tradition and stagnation on one hand and modernity and change on the other hand. As Africa is continually advocating for change through the system of modernity, *Fulani* is an example to see this advocacy at work, where what has come to be known as modernity interfaces with tradition and annihilates it, as symbolically displayed when Kamal defeats Magaji. Evidently, Kamal emerges from an environment that is anxious of modernity, while Magaji's life is confined to a place in a world untouched by the insignia of modernity. Rather, it is dominated by the persistent tropes of the pre-modern: namely custom and tradition. Therefore, the conflict between Magaji and Kamal is not only a clash of personalities, but also of two different ideologies or principles. The arrogant Magaji sees honor in previous victories and feels that any intruding opponent should be humiliated and dishonored in defeat. But the stubborn Kamal intents to show his social superiority over the man whom he judges to be an unexposed and stagnant villager. Their personalities are not complementary, as the stubborn Kamal becomes the unwitting agent for change. Socially, he is a role model. He decides to go to the village as a model to be adopted and copied.

Shift in Composition and Transmission of Verbal Utterances

Does something happen to performance when filmmakers put their hands on it? This question relates to Gadjigo's (2004:34) assertion that "when the mode of the music changes, the walls of the city shake". He seems to suggest that change is a dominant idea of art in general and film in particular, as visual imagery is a powerful form of representation in the cultural evolution. While respect for tradition is a profound characteristic of *sharo*, in the video film, the filmmaker deals with tradition intrinsically. Therefore, as he concentrates on the basics of *sharo*, it implies a shift from total submission to a soft protest. He uses the theme of perseverance to present protest and criticism about the veto power of the personnel at the helm of affairs in the film's regulation commission. As Gehrmann (2005:169) explains, one should think not exclusively of African dictatorial regimes, but of the construction of authority and power as a general pattern of human behavior. Conventionally, as a fellow *sharo* performer, Kamal should not consider Magaji as an oppressor simply because he excels in *sharo*. But Kamal departs from the normative *sharo* pattern to condemn the conservative style of the authority with the sharp weapon of a curse. As a one-time convict, he screams out rude words to Magaji. To this effect, in the film the oppressor becomes an object of ridicule and rejection, which results to an ignominious end to the authoritative personnel. By inference, the subservient filmmaker introduces a subtle change. The curse Kamal renders is an allusion manifestation that out of pressure from the government, the filmmakers have resorted to subversive activities. At the same time, events in the filmic version do not always remain loyal or accurate to the traditional conventions. Traditionally, a youth gets a girl to marry by participating in *sharo*. However, the video film does not show a marriage that comes out from *sharo*, the most common and traditional space for dating. Rather, the film shows a change and presents a new space for dating. Kamal and Maryam meet for the first time on transit and become friends before Kamal gets involved in *sharo*.

Fulani is centered on pride, rivalry and suspicion. These characteristics are ingredients of contemporary daily life, which are seen in the video film to showcase departure from the traditional. Magaji is not only surprised that none of the youths has come out to say he wants to marry Malle played by Maryam Gidado in spite of her beauty, but he is also boasting. He feels that none of the youths can contest with him. He is blowing his own trumpet by shouting and praising himself to claim he is dangerous. He is bragging about how much of a champion he is at every *sharo* he does. Within the notion of tradition, by shouting his praises and epithets himself, Magaji shows changes from the traditional code of modesty as a status quo. He does not only talk loudly and very proudly about himself, but there is also alteration in his facial expression, whilst the others listen and think of how much of losers they really are. Viewers can notice a changeover between gentlemanly conduct and uncompromising conduct. He alternates between mild or calm and violent or rough behavior. More often than not, these changes happen with the guide of the filmmaker, who has a great deal of control over what happens as Turner (1987:31) suggests.

Although there is a dance involving boys and girls with audience around to depict a typical performance event, viewers of the video film gain more than the audience of the performance. Unlike the audience, the viewer gets information on principal actors, a privilege the audience do not always have during performance in the arena where actions are centered on the main event. In the video film, viewers get detailed information not only about Kamal, but also about Karima, who is not a *sharo* performer. In addition to seeing Kamal in *sharo*, viewers see how he is brought up by a single parent because his father passed away, when he was two years old. Viewers learn about the cause of his father's death through flashback. In a performance, if an audience misses an action, he or she has no opportunity to see it because there is no provision for rewind. No matter how many times it is repeated, it is going to be the second one, as no two performances are ever exactly the same. But in the video film unlike the performance, viewers see Karima, acted by Hadiza Mohammed, depicting a role model of a woman. She shows a woman's devotion to her family, firstly to her husband when he was alive, and secondly to her children after the demise of their father. She performs her gender role according to the expectations of a woman, this is very different for a punctual performance event as in *sharo*. She shows that love is reciprocal. In the early part of the video, we see how she conceals from her children the news of the circumstance that led to their father's death because she does not want to make them feel upset as she often does. In a flashback, we see how she serves food to her husband, sits close to him, and has a conversation with him while he is eating, thereby depicting the character of Karima as a modern Hausa/Fulani woman.

The video film ends with Kamal and Malle getting married. They relocate to the city. Expectantly, the video film's conclusion depicts a wind of change is blowing and affecting the performance of *sharo*. In the past, in several Hausa/Fulani localities, largely those least exposed to outside influences, this is a deeply entrenched tradition and custom, carefully carried on from generation to generation for hundreds of years. By watching such an event in the video film, one is granted a look into a past. Although there are changes, but one is also given a partial answer to the question regarding the changes. As evidenced by Kamal and Malle, already the signs of change and the dawn of a new era are apparent because they marry and live in the city. The situation of Kamal and Malle is connected to *sharo* as it is similar to how *Fulanin gida*[17] find themselves. For the newer generation, (their offspring) largely exposed to modern education and urban influence, this is a welcome change; for the older generation, a threat of extinction from remembrance in history. Yet, this confrontation between the old and the new is an age long phenomenon taking place in every part of the world.

The video film shows a departure from the traditional fetishism in the character of Kamal. While Magaji uses charm and concoction on his whips, Kamal refuses to use any charm. Instead of taking it, he shows disbelief in charms and upholds total confidence and belief in Allah, as he confesses that he will not fall down, *in sha Allahu* (by the will of God). He further manifests allegiance to the supreme-being, as he declares that *da yardan Allah zan yi nasara* (by the will of God, I will be victorious). Evidently, the binary opposition between Magaji and Kamal depicts a departure or change from the pre-Islamic to the post-Islamic society. According to Afolayan (2014:20), such a departure is marked by the framework of the ambivalent relationship between the traditional and the modern. The video film showcases change in the procedure of challenging

---

17   In terms of settlement, the Fulani are categorized into two. Firstly, there are Fulanin Daji (Forest Fulani) who live in the forests and move from one forest to another with their cattle in search of grazing land. They are also referred to as Herdsmen in Nigeria''s present political circle. The Fulani in this category perform *sharo*. Secondly, there are the Fulanin Gida (Town Fulani) who live in towns as a result of their desire to socialize or they no longer own cattle. The Fulani in this category do not practice *sharo* anymore.

an opponent. The protocol and courtesy of *sharo* demand that challenge is made during performance and only in the performance arenas. But Kamal meets Magaji in his house and challenges him to *sharo*. Evidently, Magaji is surprised by Kamal's breach of protocol. He considers Kamal as an amateur who can only perform a very amateur performance. The video film is marked by an over-reaction. Magaji does not only get up and declares a death sentence on Kamal, but he also praises himself thus,

> Aradu sai na kashe shi
>
> Sai ya gwammace bai shigo cikin duniyar nan ba.
>
> Sai ni nan Magaji
>
> Ya gagari rugan Ardo Hammadu
>
> Ya gagari rugan Haddure
>
> Na gagari rugan Hammadu (*Fulani* 00:57:02 minutes)

> I swear I will kill him
>
> He will regret ever being born
>
> Only I Magaji is here
>
> He is unbeatable in the camp of Ardo Hammadu
>
> He is unbeatable in the camp of Haddure
>
> I am unbeatable in the camp of Hammadu

(*Fulani* 00:57:02   minutes)

Within the notion of performance, when a performer praises himself he is exhibiting an act of communication. In the case of the video film, the act of communication is not only in a specially marked mode of action, but it is also put on display and screened up to observation by the viewers. The filmmaker uses ideas that have appeared before in performance, but are new not only to the viewers, but also to the filmmaker. Afolayan (2014:28) considers this as a form of creativity and goes on to say that it becomes transformative because it involves the deepest case of being creative, as the creator changes the pre-existing style in some way. More specifically, Zahradeen's choice of both the first person pronoun *ni* (I) and the third person pronoun *ya* (He) to refer to himself is as a result of his uncompromising intentions. First, he wants to speak about him by himself. Secondly, he wants to speak about him on behalf of others, particularly the boys who have already pronounced his capabilities in *sharo* performance. Thirdly, he wants to express how unbeatable he has been; therefore, he uses the emphatic pronouns.

By way of conclusion, *Fulani* becomes transformative by introducing new rules of contest, and by implication transgressing the old rule through Kamal's concern with the projection of religious principles, particularly his emphasis to prayer,

Ya Allah da kai kaɗai na dogara

Ba ni da wata madogara sai kai

Ya Allah wannan bawa naka azzaluni ne

Kuma kai ba ka son mutane azzalumai

Kuma kai ka hana zalunci, ba ka yin zalunci

Ya Allah ka taimake ni a kan wannan bawa naka

Ka sa na zama misali a rayuwarsa

Ta yadda ba zai sake addabar na ƙasa da shi ba

Ya Allah ka taimake ni a kan wannan buri nawa

Tsarki ya tabbata gare ka Allah (*Fulani* 01:29:37 minutes)

Translation

Oh God I depend on you alone

I have no other helper except you

Oh God, this man is a wicked man

Surely you do not want wickedness

You forbid wickedness hence you are not wicked

Oh God, help me over this wicked man

Let me be an example in his life

So that he will not torment those under him

Oh God, help me to achieve my heart desires

Purity is your attribute oh God (*Fulani* 01:29:37 minutes)

Although it is neither mentioned nor seen on screen, but on account of an in-depth observation of trends of events in Kannywood industry, an official was responsible for the convictions of Adam A. Zango who takes the role of Kamal in particular and other filmmakers in general. In this case, the duel in the video film can be interpreted as a fight between an oppressive and conservative official (who refuses change because he feels he has something to conserve) versus Kamal, representing filmmakers, who feel they were tormented because they come up with a progressive change. It may be right to say that rather than projecting the traditional performance as in *sharo*, the video film shifts to employ a subversive tone, which is intended to challenge the power or influence of a government or of an established principle. Magaji in the video film represents stagnation and when Kamal defeats him in the contest it suggests that a wind of change is beginning to blow towards the surge for modernity.

Analysis of *Karen Bana* (2013)

Content of *Karen Bana* (2013)

Karen Bana (2013) relates to *dambe* (local boxing)in Hausa society. Set in a rural environment, the video film's plotlines center on a young man, Dahiru, played by Adam A. Zango, as the central character. Dahiru gets the support of his father, Mada, played by Ibrahim Sinana, to attend secular school to pursue his heart desire. Despite receiving formal education in the city, he comes back to his village, Kurmi, to face allegiance to tradition. Placed between modernity and tradition, Dahiru decides to uphold modernization even though he engages Horro in boxing in order to marry Barira, played by Maryam Booth. Barira's father, Banga-banga, is an ardent traditionalist. He is a reactionary who opposes social change by refusing to give her the chance to choose her husband between two rivals. For Horro, one of the rivals, the boxing will make history repeats itself. His father Gadanga once defeated Mada, Dahiru''s father, to marry Haule, played by Hadiza Mohammed. Now Horro feels it is his time to defeat Dahiru and marry Barira to make the circle of heroism complete. But, for Dahiru, the boxing affords him the opportunity for revenge in order to restore the reputation of his family.

Conflation of a New Form of Media and the Oral Mode

Karen Bana (2013) opens with the below off screen voice-over narration. Thus, *Karen Bana* shows a cross-media and a bond between variables of orality and the accustomed modern convention of filmmaking.

> Boxing! Dirty business! As you hear it, you know it is not an easy job. It is a dirty business while others watch others are clapping, cheering and happy when they see a man falls down, bleeding from his mouth. In one town, in a society, over the years, there has been a duel among men, engaging in boxing. Some people died, some people received money, some happiness, while some got a wife....... (Karen Bana 00:01:02 minutes).

The one minute two seconds speech is an example of how the audience listen instead of watching, showcasing a moment when speech seems to have power over images. The filmmaker uses the above oral narrative (monologue) at the beginning and it serves the purpose of summarizing the whole story in one minute. This short introduction establishes, without image on the screen, the main elements of the plot which evolves around traditional boxing. The narration is embedded in the plot with due precedence to vocal modification and modulation, the result is not a re-enactment of oral performance, but simply a case of the filmmaker''s instantaneous interplay between orality and film. It shows the competition between words and images. As Colette Piault (1994:1) asserts, "the replacement of images by oral speech or by other verbal element is still dominant in films". The oral speech is inserted into the video film and thus has no concrete autonomy. Although it does not only concur with the plotlines, it is also a sort of plus, useful and interesting. It is useful for a better understanding of the main subject of the video film, which is, of course insight into the traditional boxing performance. It is interesting because it explains the nature of metamorphosis, which the performance has undergone, a central issue in this book.

Although the introductory oral narrative is short and it is in everyday diction, its insertion more or less makes the video film depart from the performance, as it depicts what Okpewho (1990:120) refers to as "high emotive charge". In terms of vocalization, the video film showcases and enjoys a certain elevation over the ordinary narrative mode in performance. Regarding the issue of the way orality reacts with film, Kaschula (2001:xxx) maintains that there is a strong connection with oral tradition in African films. The reason for the adaptation of oral tradition in films, according to Kaschula is that it is almost the basic starting point of all modern African literature. Similarly, Okpewho (1990:12) complements this intersection as he explains that his experience has been that even within the so-called speech mode, there is usually a high poetic afflatus which frequently erupts into supportive proverbs of emotional and poetic intensity. As it is the case, *Karen Bana* is endowed with hybridity. Viewers experience this transposition by hearing an off screen soundtrack of a local boxing performance singer, late 'Dan'anace praising Wandara, a popular local boxer. The significance of the song is evident when the camera captures a boxing arena in a long shot. Boxers, drummers and the spectators set the scene and introduce the video film's narrative structure. The director uses an old song to mark a return to viewers' memory lane. It is a device to uncover the connection between the soundtrack, the image and some changes. Although connection emerges from the soundtrack and the image, there is a striking shift from the traditional boxing performance. Traditionally, boxing is a performance mainly for *mahàutaa* (butchers) only. Formerly, they usually allowed their hair to grow long and then had it plaited. In the video film, a lot of people involve in boxing not only the butchers. This development suggests that traditional boxing now involves people of different professions. It has been reshaped and it is no longer associated with the butchers only. Practically, there is also a shift from the traditional hair-do that used to characterized the boxers. The video film presents the boxers with low hair-cut and others are seen with modern style hair-cut compared to when they plaited their hair.

The use of costumes is another area characterized by shift. Traditionally, when a contest is about to start, boxers take off their normal cloth and leave only a pair of knickers or underwear on them. On top of the underwear, they wear *warki* (leather loin-cloth) which is decorated. In the video film, boxers are not only seen without underwear, but they also don't have *warki* on them. In place of traditional costumes, they wear their normal short trousers ending at the knees and other boxers wear their normal trousers. Through a long shot which frames the boxers, drummers and spectators, the viewers are able to see a full view of the three categories of people in the performance space and how they are connected to each other. Typically, in a performance space, performers and spectators interact and affect or change each other in some way. In the case of the video film under review, it is the camera that does the capturing and the interaction changes to symbolize a performance within a performance, which is reformed through a modernized form of stark lighting. The intensity, direction and quality of lighting helps to influence viewers' understanding of the characters, theme and mood. For example, viewers are able to see clearly the mood of Gadanga played by Tahir Fagge and his opponent after winning and losing a fight respectively. The camera captures Gadanga, his patron and supporters in a happy mood for his victory, and then the camera moves away from them and captures Sallau, played by Rabi'u Rikadawa, the patron of the defeated boxer, showing his annoyance and departure from the arena immediately. By the use of camera movement, his annoyance and the subsequent departure from the arena is a means by which the camera communicates to the spectators and by extension the audience of the video film that there is a problem, which needs to be solved. Immediately the camera shifts from him and captures his wife to expose two divergent opinions that depict change in cultural values. On the one hand, Haule's mother is in support of her friendship with Gadanga. On the other hand, her father is not supporting the relationship. This attitude depicts parents' parallel opinions towards the choice of their daughter's partners. The voice of Haule's mother is amplified to signify her objection to her husband's decision on who marries their daughter. This incident serves as an example of shift from the traditional norm in *Karen Bana*, especially regarding interaction between husband and wife. In the traditional norm of behavior between husband and wife, as Chamo (2012:64) states, a wife is not supposed to express her feelings to her husband directly, whether she is happy or unhappy. By implication, the norm requires her to calm her temper whenever she is speaking to her husband. *Karen Bana* does not only show a departure from this tradition, but it also upholds freedom for a woman to express her views freely to her husband, especially with regards to their daughter. Therefore, expressing positive feelings by a woman to her husband and discussing the future of their daughter is worth more than mentioning. Haule's mother means that time has come for a wife to make a contribution to any decision taken in the family. A wife is not only a bona fide member of her matrimonial family, but she is also a decision maker. Evidently, Haule maintains the decision of her mother by going out to see her suitor in spite of her father's refusal. The camera functions in two ways as they chat. First, as each character speaks, the camera focuses on him or her in a closer shot. Secondly, it captures the two characters together while one is speaking to the other to signify their unity and diversity, as they are bound by a common traditional motif. But they are very different from each other on idealism: Gadanga as an advocate of tradition verse Haule as an advocate of change. As a boxer, Gadanga is ready to face any challenge. He employs the traditional use of personal praises and boasts. They are considered as powerful expressive acts used by performers to serve as weapons under conditions of high intensity of conflict and viewers realized that bursting, pride and confidence are Gadanga's strong weapons.

Besides Gadanga as a role character who is an admirer of tradition, Mada is another character whom viewers steadily see on screen. By way of characterization, he looks fearless both in and out of the ring. Indeed, he is a boxer of fearsome dimensions. He engages in two fights and wins. The camera captures him, Haule and her father. Although they meet by coincidence, from a critical point of view, this work considers that the function of the camera is to capture a situation depicting shift from the traditional norm of *kunya* to an interaction which is not only sophisticated, but it is also comfortable in social situations. Even though Mada and Haule are not yet married, on the one hand, critics may look at the presence of Sallau as a breach of the status quo for stopping to talk to the suitor of his daughter while she is conversing with him. On the other hand, this work considers the need for in-laws to socialize with each other. When they socialize, they come together to understand each other. As a result of interacting, they will aspire to a progressive society compared to the type demonstrated by Gadanga and Mada. The dialogue between them is a testimony that Gadanga has a grudge against Mada:

Mada: Me ya kawo ka nan Gadanga?

Gadanga: Gaban filin dambe ya tashi a nan

Mada: Kaitonka Gadanda. Ka manta cewa soyayya gamon jini ne ba ƙarfi ba?

Gadanga: Haka kake gani. Ina maka gargaɗi, ka shiga taitayinka.

Mada: Gadanga! Ko za mu sa zare ne? (*Karen Ban*a 00:30:50 minutes)

Translation

Mada: What brings you here Gadanga.

Gadanga: It is the hostility in the boxing ring that turns up here.

Mada: Woe unto you Gadanga. You forget that love is an emotional contest not a physical one?

Gadanga: That is your perception. I am warning you to mind your status.

Mada: Gadanga! Can we duel? (*Karen Bana* 00:30:50 minutes)

The director makes use of both the camera and the characters to make known his intention, which is to showcase transformation in performance. The camera goes round and zooms on Gadanga, Mada, Haule and finally on Sallau who speaks directly to the camera. The appearance of Haule and Sallau in addition to Sallau using Haule (his daughter) to entice Gadanga and Mada to fight is a new development in boxing. Viewers hear him saying to her,

Ki saurare ni. Mutum yakan iya samun soyayyar mace ta ka da wani mutum a ƙasa. Mutum yakan iya samun soyayyar mace ta furucin bakinsa. Mutum yakan iya samun soyayyar mace ta basirarsa. Mutum yakan iya samun soyayyar mace ta amfani da dukiyarsa. Mutun yakan iya samun soyayyar mace ta amfani da takobi (*Karen Bana* 00:32:20 minutes).

Translation

Listen to me. A man can win a love if he knocks down his opponent to the ground. A man can win a love with his tongue. A man can win a love with his wealth. A man can win a love with his knowledge. A man can win a love with a sword (*Karen Bana* 00:32:20).

Sallau's enumeration of symbols involved in boxing such as ground, tongue and knowledge are practical and workable in traditional boxing.

But his inclusion of wealth and sword as symbols for strategies of winning is an example of the transformation in performance. It signifies that in today's boxing performance it is not unlikely that boxers use fraudulent actions to effect defeat of their opponents. When the fight gets tough, they are likely to use sharp objects on their opponents. In the video film, Gadanga does not use sharp object, but he rubs pepper into the eyes of Mada, his opponent and he eventually defeats him. It is not only against the rules of traditional boxing to do so, but it is also considered a cheat.

Karen Bana presents night shots throughout the film to reflect on challenge. Viewers see Haule and Mada in the center of the frame. When the camera fades away, viewers see Gadanga and Mada in a close shot facing each other closely. In a night shot, viewers see Gadanga at the cemetery seeking for magical powers. The choice of night by the director is not only to put emphasis on shadows that often conceal some images, but also to create a sense of mysticism. Lighting in the night scene is thoroughly planned. The setting is not entirely dark and the light does not make the setting very bright like in broad day light. The lighting crew ensures that the light has achieved its desired effect on viewers. It reminds them of the significance of grave in traditional boxing performance, which is to enhance defeat. Those who use grave as a symbol of defeat claim that when the hand of a boxer touches a dead body in the grave, and then hits an opponent, the opponent is bound to fall down. Not only do the night scenes try to uphold the tradition of local boxing, but also the praises and epithets of Gadanga and Mada and their subsequent fight. But the point of departure from the traditional is the aftermath of the fight. When Gadanga wins, Mada threatens to kill him. As a result of the threats, Mada is expelled from the community. This development shows a shift from the traditional concept of boxing as a do-or-die affair.

One important thing about *Karen Bana* is the late arrival of the two protagonists: Dahiru, played by Adam A. Zango, and Barira, played by Maryam Booth. When viewers are introduced to Dahiru, they see him going back to his village, Kurmi, after completing his studies in a modern school in the city. Few minutes of his introduction, a technique to engage viewers in the apex of the tension in the video film is set in motion by the director. While Dahiru waits for a vehicle, viewers are introduced to Barira, who is also from Kurmi. What may seem as coincidence or chance forms an essential part of the video film when Dahiru and Barira meet and board the same bus. Their introduction as persons who are meeting for the first time and the subsequent journey they embark on together are significant in the development of the plotlines in particular and the video film in general in terms of changes in cultural values. By virtue of his education and exposure, Ɗahiru will not have interest in Barira. She is not his class, his social status does not match with her manners, as the director presents her as a typical villager. Contrary to the very possible viewers' assumption, Ɗahiru and Barira develop however interest in each other. This development does not only suggest a shift from the traditional same class syndrome, but it also shows what Ɗahiru will go through. The immediate fading in of the video film's title, *Karen Bana*, on screen, the appearance of Horro, played by Tijjani Asase, and the live artist who sings his praises and epithets are manifestations of a challenge that Ɗahiru will encounter. Not only does this device remind viewers of the presence of *makaɗan maza* (singers for professionals) during boxing, but it also informs them that they are viewing a performance in a new medium. Evidently, they see the link between the performance and the video film along with some changes. In the video film, there is a departure from the use of traditional musical instruments used during boxing performance to highlight the inclusion of gadgets to reflect hybridity. Viewers see the performance announcer using microphone connected to loudspeakers in order to amplify voice, so that people from far places can hear him. This development is not by chance, as no part of the world, no human activity is untouched by the new media. Societies worldwide are being renewed for better by changes in the global media and information circulation. In this regard, it is a privilege enjoined by necessity that most social systems are affected by the dynamics of global media, particularly systems in a society which is experiencing dual influence. Inevitably, such a society must make a shift consciously or unconsciously from tradition to modernity. The arrival of Ɗahiru who might be considered as an outsider changes the status quo. It represents a timely and inevitable change in the community. He does not only become a threat to Horro, the existing village champion, but he also influences changes in Horro's uncivilized and uncompromising attitudes. He used to be feared and dreaded hence everyone in the village is afraid of him and nobody can challenge him. This shows how physical strength, as exhibited by Horro, can no longer be a determining factor in the society. Therefore, the concept of the Hausa proverb, *mai ƙarfi sarkin ƙauye* (in the village, a strong man is the king) is changed, as nowadays there are constituted authorities that deal with conflicts in civilized manners. From the foregoing changes, a rethinking about hostility between Horro and 'Dahiru, as they interact, is instilled. Interaction is essential in the maintenance and transmission of culture. It comes into being when each of at least two participants is aware of the presence of the other and each has reason to believe the other is similarly aware. In such a situation, different kinds of actions are involved including use of language, non-speech actions like facial expression and body movement.

For example, the camera shows Horro coming conceitedly in slow motion. As soon as he meets 'Dahiru for an interaction, normal coverage resumes, and the camera captures him communicating with 'Dahiru (*Karen Bana* 00: 59:28 minutes). On one hand, this situation shows how Horro is enthusiastic about a child's obedience to parents, as well as how parents show allegiance to culture in the traditional way. He heeds to the conviction of his father with passion and without questioning. On the other hand, 'Dahiru deviates from the tradition and injects change. It is possible due to his acquisition of secular education, as it is the prerequisite of any meaningful social change. In the words of Vetinde (2012:471), "education is not only at the heart of the transformations that African societies are experiencing now, it is the linchpin of the continent's development [....] It is hard to think about the changing African societies without envisioning an appropriate form of education". Thus, the character of 'Dahiru supports the view of Walter J. Ong (1982:ix) that "modes and categories influenced from the past no longer seem to fit the reality experienced by a new generation". 'Dahiru is critical of the application of some rules or systems and he sets out to change them radically. 'Dahiru's opinion on child and father relationship diverges from that of Horro. His concern about some hidden issues in their family does not only represent a transition in the physical and mental development of a child, but it also manifests transition in the rapport between father and child. From the traditional point of view, children must not question their parents on any decision they take. In *Karen Bana,* 'Dahiru does not only persist in asking his parents, but he also challenges them to tell him what transpired between his father and Gadanga. By implication, time has changed, people also have to change and walk according to time, as a Hausa proverb says, *zamani riga* (literally, time is a gown and it is worn accordingly). It means that things are done according to time. Therefore, in this generation, people allow their wards to share their experiences. To this effect, the director shows 'Dahiru sharing his father's agony when the video film cuts back to flashback shots, a manifestation of his transition from childhood to manhood.

Banga-banga is another character that the director uses to show an example of a typical allegiance to culture and tradition. But his ideas are entirely contrary to the opinions of his wife, who continuously opposes the archaic and conservative ideas of her husband. While he insists on tradition, she is concerned about their reputation as parents. To him, as a boxer, it is against the tradition of boxing to allow his daughter to get married without a contest being performed among her suitors. On the other hand, his wife opposes boxing because she does not want any shameful thing in their family, should the contest become calamitous. She challenges her husband's authority as the head of the family even though he presses hard on his wish by stating that whether she likes it or not, the fight must take place because it is their old tradition (*Karen Bana* 01:28:58 minutes). Evidently, there are two divergent opinions here. While Banga-banga is influenced by tradition and custom, his wife indicates that she is shifting from tradition to modernity. It could be right to say that Banga-banga's consistent allegiance to tradition and the persistent disagreement with his wife is an instance of what Vetinde (2012:464) says about Africa in dealing with the process of transformation. Banga-banga seems to negotiate his stand and safeguard his unchanging and uncompromising ideology around the question, which Vetinde (2012:464) asked sarcastically - how much of a people's culture and value systems should be sacrificed on the alter of national progress? This scenario brings out the cultural disparity between Banga-banga and his wife. He is faced with the challenge of adjusting to changing times. With his traditional allegiance, he seems not to be apt in dealing and or compromising with the shifting cultural realities. His concern for a real or genuine Hausa, to borrow Vetinde (2012:484) phrase, "cultural purity" in this era of cultural globalization may not only be unrealistic but also unreliable. Indeed, he and his wife are two completely different individuals in character and principles. While he seems to be primeval in thoughts and acts, as he shows concern for traditional rules, his wife does not only insist on change, but she also carries on with her innovative ideas. By inference, there is need for a modern society in which the will of necessity transcends tradition, whereby the people will have to embody change and choose between traditional allegiance and transformation.

Karen Bana depicts acts linked to fetishism and shifts from it. The concept of the fetish relates to an object, which is believed to have supernatural powers. Specifically, it is a man-made object that possesses power over other objects. The use of charms, enchantment, juju and offensive witchcraft are associated with religious fetishism, which this work is concerned with. It is commonly used in traditional religious beliefs, as opposed to Karl Marx's commodity fetishism, although Marx picked up the word from its erstwhile meaning. In *Karen Bana*, characters who take the role of boxers are seen with armlets during boxing. Its major function is to enhance victory. Similarly, in one of the scenes, Haule finds Horro at night seeking magical powers in addition to Gadanga's fetish behavior, which the director presents earlier. The director's persistence in repeating the act is to show that fetishism is practiced among boxers. According to Madauci, Isa and Daura (1968:73), as it was the case, every boxer had his *boka* (traditional healer) who prepares his charm. More often than not, they exceed the limit of religious principles, such as performing all sorts of rites under the tamarind tree, all in the search for excellence. On one hand, the director's persistence on acts of fetishism is to indicate its reality. On the other hand, his persistence goes hand in hand with a critical point of departure from fetishism. The video film evidently suggests that fetishism is shifting and nowadays many people do not only condemn it, but they also do not believe in it. For example, Mada says he has a strong belief in Allah with whom everything is possible and he does not fear any magic or enchantment. Secondly, his son Dahiru does not get involved in acts linked to fetishism when he engages Horro in boxing. Rather, he approaches the fight systematically. He does not only undergo rigorous training, but he also acquires some skills and techniques which are synonymous with modern boxing. In addition, the director does not only use the character of Haule as a symbol of metamorphosis, but he also portrays her as an example of a woman of her words and a passionate advocate of change. For example, when she meets Horro at the point of an act linked to fetishism, the situation makes her to change her allegiance to tradition. As a young woman, she too passes through the same tradition, but now as an adult, she has a different opinion about it. She has good reasons to sideline her allegiance to tradition. She considers Horro's fetishism as devilish and when he uses it, it is actually bound to kill

'Dahiru. She feels there is no point sticking to a tradition that will jeopardize the future and entire life of a young graduate, whose father suffered to educate him so that he will be of great help to the community. Like Haule, Barira and 'Dahiru's friend are advocates of change. Their position on boxing for a wife shows that as youths they have a common ideology that shifts from the conservative view of tradition. To them, even though 'Dahiru is man enough to wipe away the pains his father suffers and then restore his lost prestige, they feel it should be done in a civilized manner that will not be at the detriment of his life. Their decision is a departure from Mada's character as a stalwart of an eye for an eye-revenge. In addition to 'Dahiru's friend and Barira's acts of change, Mada's wife finds his decision not only uncompromising, but also unforgivable. To her, there is no reason that supports the fight. Therefore, they should not destroy their son just to fulfill their wishes. The video film does not only depict Mada facing questions about the significance of tradition, but also reminds him of its obsolescence. His insistence on tradition is a case in point. He has to consider the relevance of discarded tradition. The character of Haule does not only inform him, but it also intimidates him. In other words, the older generation is destined to relinquish its traditional role, as the video film reveals. This development is inevitable and it is hastened by a technologically changing world where the conservatives may feel that they are continuously getting outdated. As James Monaco (2000:72) reckons on technology, he emphasizes that, "recording technology now offers us the opportunity of capturing a representation of sounds, images, and events and transmitting them directly to the observer within the necessary interposition of the artist's personality and talents". This can be realized in the ring during the grand finale when viewers hear on screen live boxing songs and see spectators and boxers. Horro and 'Dahiru are placed in the center of the camera and a live artist is praising them. The on screen song gives way for an off screen repeated mentioning of the video film's title *Karen Bana*, warning Horro that 'Dahiru, the *Karen Bana,* (the protagonist) will deal with Horro, the *Birin Zamani* (the antagonist). The video film's adaptation of the Hausa proverb, *Karen bana shi ne maganin birin zamani* (a monkey is no match to a dog) as its title is by all means exploiting and exposing the power of orality. In addition, it exposes two divergent opinions. There are conflicting views between those who uphold allegiance to custom and tradition, on one hand, and those who feel that tradition is archaic and must be discarded by switching allegiance, on the other hand. This development suggests that culture is dynamic. It has the power and the capacity for change or transformation of social structures that are highlighted and made manifest to the society through the performances under review. The issue of change or transformation can be seen in the final fight between Dahiru, a graduate, and Horro, a stark illiterate. While Dahiru represents modernity and change, Horro represents tradition and stagnation. Dahiru's victory is a symbol of modernity prevailing over tradition. At the end of the video film, viewers see Horro hailing Dahiru. This gesture does not only indicate that Horro has overcome tradition, but now he is also an admirer of change in their society. Finally, Dahiru's migration to the city shows that unless we come closer to cosmopolitan life, we cannot interact and integrate.

The use of proverbs in the video film's storylines plays a great role in depicting the status of orality in the society. In about three minutes of fierce dialogue between two characters, Gadanga and Mada, five proverbs are employed such as *sai an gwada akan san na kwarai* (a quality of something is known only by testing it) (*Karen Bana* 01:55:47 minutes), *barewa ba ta yi gudu danta ya yi rarrafe ba* (the manner someone behaves is the same manner his or her children will behave) (*Karen Bana* 01:56:09 minutes), *dan da ya yi wa da'ira tirken wawa* (woe to the son who is used to the ring, but fails to defeat a beginner) (*Karen* Bana 01:56:28 minutes), *karen bana shi ne maganin birin zamani* (a monkey is no match to a dog) (*Karen Bana* 01:57:38 minutes), *fankan fankan ba shi ne kilishi ba* (strength is better than size in fight) (*Karen Bana* 01:57:51 minutes). In Hausa society, the use of proverbs is very common in everyday speech. Users of proverbs sometimes play on words and render the referent sarcastic as seen in *Karen Bana*. While they come in what people say and do, they also express the wisdom of the speaker and expose the tradition of the people at the same time showing communicative mechanism. However, in the video film, proverbs are embedded not only in speech, but also in action, as it is often said that action speaks louder than voice. The action helps to emphasize the strength of what the actor aims at saying in the proverb. *Karen Bana* therefore exemplifies the fusion between the genres of orality and cinema and serves a good example of this unification.

Conclusion

The video films in the corpus cannot be regarded as imitations of Bollywood, as a section of the society often considers them. Rather, they are Kannywood. They may not be the video films that the *Hisbah*, the pro-Sharia militia in Kano thought of silencing because of actresses and actors in body contact depicting promiscuous act. Rather, they are video films based on Hausa oral tradition. *Karen Bana's* success as the best video film in an award presentation in Kano is a testimony. In these films familiar narratives depicting cultural motifs abound. In the case of the use of a folktale, for instance, the story as oral narration is already packed in the memory of filmmakers and viewers alike, making it sound more genuine than what would be invented over-night. Evidently, as filmmakers will continue producing cultural video films, viewers will continue to cherish them and this will determine the future of Kannywood industry. This does not necessarily require all viewers grasping all the video films. If one can produce ten video films and only a few messages in just some few of the video films are found useful, something is achieved. Filmmakers should not expect that all the contents of their video films must be accepted. If viewers make use of the message in just one scene in a video film, the aim of the filmmaker is achieved. For instance, folktales and video films bring to limelight the issue of attitudes such as the opinions and feelings that people usually have towards certain things and how they relate to those things. For example, the result of tolerance and obedience as shown by Hama's daughter in *Ruwan Bagaja* relates to horse riding, drumming, music, escorts and perfume. All these are associated with royalty, which indicates an upper class in the society. Things like leprosy, flies, insects and riding on donkey as done by Larai's daughter are synonymous with poverty stricken condition hence they are looked at contemptuously and negatively in the society. Basically, filmmakers produce video films in order to educate, entertain viewers or to bring up something into the glare of publicity. In achieving this goal, therefore, Kannywood filmmakers use traditional performances as sources of their plotlines. Some viewers do not know some of the performances, but as they are now being transported into video films, they are beginning to experience them. For those who know them, the transported video films serve as a way of revisiting them. If Kannywood filmmakers will continue to use traditional performances of the distant past, they will not only contribute on revitalizing eroded performances, but they will also uncover the changes in cultural values.

7 GENERAL CONCLUSIONS

This research investigated African traditional theatre in contemporary films, the manner the films manifest how culture is captured and the transformation that has occurred thereafter (the metamorphosis of performance, oral heritage and medial transformation that has occurred in films). The focus is on Kannywood video films, which are broadly conceptualized as video films in Nigeria, with close reference to Kano, northern Nigeria, in the Hausa language. Prior to the introduction of the video films, performances in the arena formed the principal means of entertainment. But due to development in technology and globalization, they are transformed or shifted and today's Kannywood video films do not only consist of scenes of these performances, but are also based on performances such as folktale, *tashe, dambe, sharo and bori*. More specifically, the work identified some changes in the course of the emergence of the Kannywood film industry. These include the crossover from theatre to the cinema, the transformation of actors and actresses from stage to screen. It is posited that there has been a shift from the use of the video camera in television stations to the video industry.

The analysis has indicated that elements of metamorphosis are enshrined in the video films' actions and narratives to eschew tradition and to affirm the force of modernization. To give but some examples: It is evident in my findings that Mada's persistence in *Karen Bana* (2013) that his daughter must get married in the traditional way, contrary to his wife's opinion, is an example of film being an artistic space for exposing a conservative and male dominated society. In the same manner, my findings indicate that, Kamal's relocation back to the city in *Fulani* (2012) despite his initial desire to go back to his roots, is an example of a changing society which embodies modern lifestyle which is not only envisaged and enticing, but it is also valued.

In shifting performances to video films, innovative film narration is realized through technical devices such as the creative matching of images and sounds. The question now is: After all the modes of transformation, especially the manipulation of the camera, what happens to the original performance? It seems to have faded, but my findings have shown that it has not only been absorbed by a new medium, but it has also become a collective, reorganized finished product, the concentrated essence of cultural significance that has acted upon the original performance. As Turner (1987:31) explains, viewers can now speak of such new and transformed performances as having a creative life of their own. It has this quality-record of the director's manipulation of the camera. Being a new product, in terms of storage systems, video films outlast oral performance. And with regards to viewing, while performance in the arena can be repeated many times, each time being unique and different from the others, a performance in a video film is not only a transformed performance, but it is also a permanent record on VHS tape and on disc respectively.

Although almost all the techniques of filmmaking which Kannywood filmmakers use have been adopted from the western world, the filmmakers have been able to create video films on local performances with very original film language and strong local characteristics. These are the types of video films, which this work has discussed. The filmmaker's video film language is Hausa, understood by Hausa and marked by the oral tradition. The filmmakers have been initiated into oral tradition and to the narrative forms of the storyteller / performer. While the storyteller / performer uses words and body language, as the study has shown, the filmmaker uses words, body language via the actors and images to convey meaning. He has also at his disposal a much more varied medium to transmit his message: technical means of production, special audiovisual effects, the images of the actors, their movements and, obviously, the sound. He uses all these ingredients to speak to his audience and to give the narration the appearance of change. The filmmaker's raw material is not the spoken word, as in the communication between storyteller and audience, but rather images and language. The words of the storyteller are translated into images. This is all the more necessary as the film will be viewed by audiences with different linguistic backgrounds. Despite the changes, since the video films are rooted or developed from or strongly influenced by orality, quite naturally, they reflect the filmmaker's cultural identity. Based on this, as a rule, the oral tradition marks the structure as well as the content of the films. The films' narratives are not only structured in a linear pattern, but they usually illustrate a moral teaching.

The book has shown that Kannywood filmmakers have produced many video films in the two and half decades of inception despite the technical, political and financial difficulties they encounter. Just the same way the video films have different genres, their themes also vary. But the ones which are analyzed in this work do not only reflect conventional performance, but they also represent realities that are gradually evolving. Specifically noticeable in this regard are the scenes that integrate and represent both conventional and hybrid cultural norms.

The represented society in Kannywood video films is characterized by change, which the filmmakers present adjacent to the existing situations. The study has shown the harmony between orature and technology, as created through the imported film medium. The new medium is integrated into the existing traditional and cultural environment where local narrative traditions have been adapted into the global film medium to show Hausa cum African cultural transformations. Therefore, the work highlighted that Kannywood filmmakers have embraced both Western, Indian and African influences, which are in line with contemporary medial culture. The challenge now is for the filmmakers to extend their creativity beyond the borders of Hausa speaking domains. As the primary use of language is to communicate, Kannywood filmmakers can use wider and globally accepted language to subtitle the dialogues using their linguistic competences. It is possible that the use of new and modern technologies along with subtitling might create the conditions for a larger audience. While some of the video films can be accessed on youtube, many of them (especially the ones I used for the analysis of this work) could not be found on youtube, and could not be viewed by a laptop because they are not in compatible formats and they could not be converted as well. Thus, technical quality remains a major problem that requires great attention.

Concerning northern Nigeria, which remains the central space for Kannywood, it should be kept in mind that it has always been a part of a global society, at least in the older sense of the term. In this regard, I would like to refer to D. W. Mckiernan's (2008:158), work on cinema and community. Mckiernan quotes Massey's idea of a global sense of place that, "despite all the shifts to our conception of place brought about by globalization, it is important to remember that places do have uniqueness". It is clear that much more attention specifically technical and the film's diegesis need to be given to Kannywood as a contemporary variant of Nigeria film industry. If the government can guarantee adequate enabling environment for the filmmakers, the actors and actresses, the industry will not only develop well or vigorously, but it will also be an avenue for more revenue for Nigeria, especially now that the price of crude oil tumbles in the international market.

Kannywood video films' substandard quality notwithstanding, the industry survives the obnoxious short-comings and problems. Despite the occurring deficiencies or weaknesses, Kannywood remains a huge area for research not only in the fields of literature, film studies and culture, but also in anthropology, linguistics, sociology and religion. The video films can offer researchers the opportunity to investigate the different aspects of the industry such as production and marketing. There is enough in the video films for scholars or researchers who are interested in the contemporary Hausa/African society and how the society is represented in the films that are produced by indigenous filmmakers. Specifically, this work recommends that the aesthetics of language, such as the beauty, ugly, comic, as applicable to the films' diegesis is an area for further research.

FILMOGRAPHY

Borin Ibro. Director: Auwal Y. Abdullahi. Albashir Productions, Kano. 2008.

Dawayya. Director: Bala Anas Babillata. Iyan-Tama Multimedia, Kano. 2001.

Jakadiya. Director: Aminu Saira. Kabugawa Production, Kano. 2011.

Karen Bana. Director: Falalu Dorayi. Prince Zango Productions Nigeria Ltd, Kaduna. 2013.

Ruwan Bagaja. Director: Iliyasu Abdulmumini. Nautica Productions, Kano. 1998.

Sangaya. Director: Aminu Muhammed Sabo. Sarauniya Films, Kano. 2000

Tashe. Director: Hamisu Yusuf. A. E. Production. Kano. 2010.

Fulani. Director: Mu''azzam Idi Yari. Amart Entertainment, Kano. 2012

Masha Allah. Director: Bashir Abdullahi Rijau. Grafarts Consultants Ltd and 3sp International Ltd. Jos. 2008.

Hajiya Babba. Director: Iliyasu Abdulmumini. Barumi MoviesFilms. Kano. 2015.

Waraka. Director: Bala Anas Babinlata. Klassique Films. Kano. 2004.

Zaman Gida. Director: Ismail Khalil Ja''in. Sky Entertainment. Kano. 2010.

Rabin Jiki. Director: Yasin Auwal. UK Entertainment. Kano. 2011.

Matar Jami''a. Director: Yasin Auwal. 17/18 Motion Pictures Enterprises. Kano. 2013.

Mazan ko Matan. Director: Bello Muhammad Bello. Hamrahz Production, Jos. 2010.

Bana Bakwai. Director: Falalu Dorayi. FKD Productions. Kano. 2007.

Dijangala. Director: Ali Nuhu. FKD Productions. Kano. 2008.

Hubbi. Director: Ali Nuhu. Prince Zango Nigeria Ltd. Kaduna. 2012.

Gabar Cikin Gida. Director: Yakubu Mohammed. 2 Effects Empire. Abuja. 2013.

*Turmin Danya*Director: Salisu Galadanci. The Tumbin Giwa Drama Group. Kano. 1990.

Shaihu Umar. Director: Adamu Halilu. Nigerian Film Corporation. Jos. 1976.

Kasarmu Ce. Director: Sadik Abubakar Balewa. N. F. T. S. Beacons field. 1991.

Sarauniya Aminatu. Director: Nasiru B. Muhammad. 2005.

Zaurawa. Director: Ali Gumzak. Maiƙwai MoviesFilms. Kano. 2013.

BIBLIOGRAPHY

Abdullahi, Aliyu II (Ed). *Fim*. Kaduna: Informart Publishers Ltd, 161 Edition, May 2013.

Abraham, Roy Clive. *Dictionary of the Hausa Language*. London: Hodder and Stroughton, 1964.

Abu-Manga, Al-amin. *Hausa in the Sudan: Process of Adaptation to Arabic*. Cologne: Rüdiger Köppe Verlag, 1999.

Adamu, Abdalla Uba., Adamu, Yusuf M. & Jibril, U. F. Eds. *Hausa Home Videos:Technology, Economy and Society*. Kano: Centre for Hausa Cultural Studies, 2004.

Adamu, Abdalla Uba. *Read to Reel: Transformation of Hausa Popular Literature from Orality to Visuality*. Unpublished Paper Presented at the 24 International Convention of the Association of Nigerian Authors, held on 11 - 12 November, 2005 at the Murtala Muhammad Library Complex, Kano, 25 pages.

Adamu, Abdalla Uba. *Transglobal Media Flows and African Popular Culture: Revolution and Reaction in Muslim Hausa Popular Culture*. Kano: Visually Ethnographic Productions, 2007.

Adamu, Abdalla Uba. *Annotated Bibliography of Criticisms Against Hausa Prose Fiction*. Posted in the internet Saturday, March 17, 2007.http://arewanci.blogspot.com/2007/03/annotated-biblio graphy-of-criticisms-html last accessed June 21, 2017.

Adamu, Abdalla Uba. "Breaking Out, Speaking Out: Youth, Islam and the Production of Indigenous Hausa Literature in Northern Nigeria" In *Beyond the Language Issue: The Production, Mediation and Reception of Creative Writing in African Languages.* Ed. Anja Oed. Köln: Rüdiger Köppe Verlag, 2008, p. 209-220.

Adamu, Abdalla Uba. "Islam, Hausa Culture and Censorship in Nigerian Video Film." In: *Viewing African Cinema in the Twenty First Century*. Eds. Saul Mahir and Austen Ralph A. Ohio: Ohio University Press, 2010, p. 63-73.

Adamu, Abdalla Uba. "Transnational Flows and Local Identities in Muslim Northern Nigerian Films: From Dead Poets Society Through

Mohabbatein to So....." In *Popular Media, Democracy and Development in Africa*. Ed. Herman Wasserman. London: Routledge, 2010, p. 223-234.

Adamu, Abdalla Uba. "Media Technologies and Literary Transformations in Hausa Oral Literature" In *From Oral Literature to Video: The Case of Hausa*. Eds. Joseph McIntyre & Mechthild Reh. Köln: Rüdiger Köppe Verlag, 2011, p. 45-80.

Adamu, Abdalla Uba. *An Ethnographic History of Kannywood – The Hausa Video Film Industry*. Unpublished Paper Presented at the Kano State Film Festival, March 18, 2013, Kano: Nigeria, 2013, 20 pages.

Adekoya, Olusegun. "Love's Metamorphosis in Third-Generation African Women's Writing. The Example of Lola Shoneyin's *The Secret of Baba Segi's Wives*." In Tradition and Change in Contemporary West and East African Fiction. Ed. Ogaga Okuyade. Amsterdam-New York: Rodopi. 2014, p. 333- 363.

Adesanya, Afolabi. "From Film to Video." In *Nigerian Video Films*. Revised and Expanded Edition. Ed. Jonathan Haynes. Athens: Ohio University Centre for International Studies. (Africa Series. No. 73), 2000, p. 37-50.

Adesokan, Akin. "How They See it: The Politics and Aesthetics of Nigerian Video Films." In *African Drama and Performance*. Eds. Conteh-Morgan John and Olaniyan Tejumola. Bloomington: Indiana University Press, 2004, p.189-197.

Ahmad, Ado. "Hausa Love Stories: Origins, Development and their Im pact on the Hausa in Nigeria." In *From Oral Literature to Video: The Case of Hausa*. Eds. Joseph McIntyre & Mechthild Reh. Köln: Rüdiger Köppe Verlag, 2011, p.1-44.

Ahmad, Ado. "Littattafan Soyayya: Samuwarsu da Bunk"asarsu da Kuma Tasirinsu ga Al'ummar Hausawa a Nijeriya". In *From Oral Literature to Video:The Case of Hausa*. Eds. Joseph McIntyre & Mechthild Reh. Köln: Rüdiger Köppe Verlag, 2011, p. 1-44.

Ahmad, Gausu. "The Response of Kano Ulama to the Phenomenon of the Hausa Home Video: Some Preliminary Observations." In *Hausa*

Home Videos: Technology, Economy and Society. Eds. Abdalla Uba Adamu, Yusuf M. Adamu and Umar Faruk Jibrin. Kano: Centre for Hausa Cultural Studies, 2004, p. 142-153.

Ahmad, Sa'idu 'Ba6ura. "From Oral to Visual: The Adaptation of Daskin .Da-Ridi to Home Video." In *Hausa Home Videos: Technology, Economy and Society.* Eds. Adalla Uba Adamu, Yusuf M. Adamu and Umar Faruk Jibrin. Kano: Centre for Hausa Cultural Studies, 2004, p. 154-161.

Ahmad, Sa''idu 'Ba6ura. "From Orality to Mass Media: Hausa Literature in Northern Nigeria." In *Interfaces between the Oral and the Written.* Eds. Alain Ricard & Flora Veit-Wild. Amsterdam: Rodopi, 2005, p. 219-231.

Ahmed, Umaru Balarabe. *The Poverty of Knowledge: Essays at Sixty.* Zaria: Dayo Habeeb Press, 2000.

Ahmed, Umaru Balarabe. *The Taxonomy of Hausa Drama.* Zaria: Ahmadu Bello University, 1985.

Ali, Bashir. "Historical Review of Films and Hausa Drama, and their Impact on the Origin, Development and Growth of Hausa Home Videos in Kano." In *Hausa Home Videos: Technology, Economy and Society.* Eds. Abdalla Uba Adamu, Yusuf M. Adamu and Umar Faruk Jibrin. Kano: Centre for Hausa Cultural Studies, 2004, p. 25-45.

Andrew, Dudley. "Adaptation" In *Film Adaptation.* Ed. James Naremore. London: The Athlone Press, 2000, p. 28-37.

Animasaun, Kayode. *NoSRA THEORY On Gazesetting and Analysis of Nollywood Movies.* Ibadan: Kraft Books Limited, 2011.

Asaduddin, M. and Amuradha Ghosh. "Filming Fiction: Some Reflections and a Brief History" In Asaduddin M. and Amuradha Ghosh. Eds. *Filming Fiction: Tagore, Premchand, and Ray.* New Delhi: Oxford University Press, 2012. p. xiii-xxxi.

Ayakoroma, Barclays Foubiri. *Trends in Nollywood: A Study of Selected Genres.* Ibadan: Kraft Books Limited, 2014.

Bailey, Carol A. *A Guide to Qualitative Field Research* Second Edition. London: Pine Forge Press, 2007.

Barber, Karin: John, Collins and Ricard, Alain. *West African Popular Theatre*. Bloomington: Indiana University Press, 1997.

Bargery, George Percy. *A Hausa-English Dictionary and English-Hausa Vocabulary*. London: Oxford University Press, 1934.

Bauman, Richard. *Verbal Art as Performance*. Illinois: Waveland Press, INC, 1977.

Baumann, Richard. *Story, Performance and Event: Contextual Studies of Oral Narratives.* Cambridge: Cambridge University Press, 1986.

Bauman, Richard. Ed. *Folklore, Cultural Performances, and Popular Entertainments*. New York: Oxford University Press, 1992.

Bauman, Richard. "Performance." In: *Folklore, Cultural Performances, and Popular Entertainments*. Ed. Richard Bauman. New York: Oxford University Press, 1992, p. 41-49.

Bazin, Andre. "Adaptation, or the Cinema as Digest" In *Film Adaptation.* Ed. James Naremore. London: The Athlone Press, 2000. p. 19 – 27.

Becker, Heike. "Nollywood in Urban Southern Africa: Nigerian Video Films and Their Audiences in Cape Town and Windhoek." In *Global Nollywood: The Transnational Dimensions of an African Video Filme Industry*. Eds. Matthias Krings and Onookome Okome. Bloomington: Indiana University Press, 2013, p.179-198.

Ben-Amos, Dan. "Folktale." In *Folklore, Cultural Performances, and Popular Entertainments*. Ed. Richard Bauman. New York: Oxford University Press, 1992, p. 101-118.

Cham, Mbaye. "Film and History in Africa: A Critical Survey of Current Trends and Tendencies." In *Focus on African Films*. Ed. Francoise Pfaff. Bloomington: Indiana University Press, 2004, p. 48-68.

Chamo, Isa Yusuf. *The Changing Code of Communication in Hausa Films*. Unpublished PhD Dissertation submitted to The Faculty of Oriental Studies, University of Warsaw. 2012, 161 pages.

Chutchins, Dennis. "Bakhtin, Translation and Adaptation" In *Translation and Adaptation in Theatre and Film.* Ed. Katja Krebs. London: Routledge, 2014, p. 36 – 62.

Dakata, Zulkifl A.G. "Alienation of Culture: A Menace Posed by the Hausa Home Video." In *Hausa Home Videos: Technology, Economy and Society.* Eds. Abdalla Uba Adamu, Yusuf M. Adamu and Umar Faruk Jibrin. Kano: Centre for Hausa Cultural Studies, 2004, p. 250-254.

Dasylva, Ademola O. "Con-textuality and Continuity in Nigeria." In *African Oral Literature*: *Functions in Contemporary Contexts.* Ed. Rusell Kaschula. Cape Town: New Africa Education (NAE). 2001, p. 181-190.

Diakhate, Ousmane and Eyoh, Hansel Ndumbe. "Of Inner Roots and External Adjuncts." In *The World Encyclopedia of Contemporary Theatre.* Ed. Don Rubin. Vol. 3, London and New York: Routledge. 1997, p. 17-29.

Djedje, Jacqueline Cogdell. *Fiddling in West Africa: Touching the Spirit in Fulbe, Hausa, and Dagbamba.* Bloomington: Indiana University Press, 2008.

Dobronravine, Nikolai (2003) Hausa Ajami Literature and Script: Colonial Innovations and Post- Colonial Myths in Northern Nigeria. Paper presented at Institute for the Study of Islamic Thought in Africa (ISITA), Program of African Studies (PAS) Northwestern University, International Colloquium,16-19 May, 2002.

Edkvist, Ingela. *The Performance of Tradition*: *An Ethnography of Hira Gasy Popular Theatre in Madagascar.* Stockholm: Gotab, 1997.

Frederic, Noy. "Hausa Video & Sharia Law." In *Nollywood: The Video Phenomenon in Nigeria.* Ed. Pierre Barrot. Ibadan: HEBN Publishers Plc, 2008, p. 78-89.

Furniss, Graham. *Poetry, Prose and Popular Culture in Hausa.* Washington, D. C. : Smithsonian Institution Press, 1996.

Gadjigo, Samba. "Ousmane Sembene and History on the Screen: A Look Back to the Future." In *Focus on African Films.* Ed. Francoise Pfaff. Bloomington: Indiana University Press, 2004, p. 33-47.

Gehrmann, Susanne. 2005. "Written Orature in Senegal: From the Traditionalistic Tales of Birago Diop to the Subversive Novels of Boubacar Boris Diop." In *Interfaces between the Oral and the Written: Versions and Subversions in African Literatures 2*. Eds. Alain Ricard & Flora Veit-Wild. Amsterdam: Rodopi, 2005, p. 157-180.

Geiger, Jeffrey and Rutsky, R. L. Eds. *Film Analysis: A Norton Reader. Second Edition.* New York: W. W. Norton and Company. 2013.

Geschiere, Peter: Meyer, Birget and Pels, Peter. Eds. 2008. *Readings in Modernity in Africa*. Bloomington: Indiana University Press.

Have, Paul ten. "Ethnomethodology." In *Qualitative Research Practice*. Eds. Clive Seale et al. London: Sage Publications, 2004, p. 151-164.

Haynes, Jonathan. Ed.. *Nigerian Video Films*. Revised and Expanded Edition. Athens: Ohio University Centre for International Studies (Africa Series No. 73), 2000.

Helfield, Gillian. „I' y ava' t un' fois (Once Upon a Time): Films as Folktales in Que'be'cois Cine'ma Direct" In Sharon R. Sherman and Mikel J. Koven. Eds. *Folklore / Cinema: Popular Film as Vernacular Culture*. Utah: Utah State University Press, 2007. p.10-30

Jaggar, Philip J. *Hausa*. Amsterdam: John Benjamin Publishing Company, 2001.

Jeffers, Jennifer M. *Hollywood's Appropriation of British Literature*. New York: Palgrave Macmillan, 2006.

Johnson, Dul. "Culture and Art in Hausa Video Films." In *Nigerian Video Films*. Revised and Expanded Edition. Ed. Jonathan Haynes. Athens: Ohio University Centre for International Studies. (Africa Series No. 73), 2000, p. 200-208.

Joubert, Annekie. *The Power of Performance: Linking Past and Present in Hananwa and Lobedu Oral Literature*. Berlin: Mouton de Gruyter, 2004

Juvan, Marko. *Histories and Poetics of Intertextuality*. West Lafayette: Purdue University Press, 2008.

Kaschula, Russell H. "Oral Literature in Contemporary Contexts." In *African Oral Literature: Functions in Contemporary Contexts*. Ed. Kaschula Russell H. Cape Town: New Africa Education (NAE), 2001, p. xi-xxvi.

Ker, David. *African Popular Theatre*. London: James Currey, 1995.

Kofoworola, E.O. 1981. "Traditional Forms of Hausa Drama." In *Drama and Theatre in Nigeria: A Critical Source Book*. Ed. Ogunbiyi Yemi. Lagos: The Pitman Press (Nigeria Magazine), 1981, p. 164-180.

Koven, Mikel J. *Film, Folklore, and Urban Legends*. Lanham, Maryland: The Scarecrow Press, Inc, 2008.

Krings, Matthias. "From Possession Rituals to Video Dramas: Some Observations of Dramatis Personae in Hausa Performing Arts." In *Hausa Video Films: Technology, Economy and Society*. Eds. Abdalla Uba Adamu, Yusuf M. Adamu and Umar Faruk Jibrin. Kano: Centre for Hausa Cultural Studies, 2004, p. 162- 170.

Krings, Matthias. "Nollywood Goes East: The Localization of Nigerian Video Films in Tanzania." In *Viewing African Cinema in the Twenty-First Century*. Eds. Saul Mahir and Austen Ralph A. Athens: Ohio University Press, 2010, p. 74-91.

Larkin, Brian. "Hausa Dramas and the Rise of Video Culture in Nigeria." In *Nigerian Video Films*. Revised and Expanded Edition. Ed. Jonathan Haynes. Athens: Ohio University Centre for International Studies. (Africa Series No. 73), 2000, p. 209-257.

Larkin, Brian. "Indian Films and Nigerian Lovers: Media and the Creation of Parallel Modernities." In *Readings in African Popular Fiction*. Ed. Stephanie Newell. Bloomington: Indiana University Press, 2002, p, 18-32.

Larkin, Brian. "From Majigi to Hausa Video Films: Cinema and Society in Northern Nigeria". In *Hausa Home VideosHausa video films: Technology, Economy and Society*. Eds. Abdalla Uba Adamu, Yusuf M. Adamu and Umar Faruk Jibrin. Kano: Centre for Hausa Cultural Studies, 2004, p. 46-53.

Larkin, Brian. "Degraded Images, Distorted Sounds: Nigerian Video & the Infrastructure of Piracy." In *Readings in Modernity in Africa*. Eds. Peter Geschiere, Birgit Meyer and Peter Pels. Bloomington: Indiana University Press, 2008, p. 146-155.

Lawan, Yusuf Aliyu (Ed). *Muntaz*. Kano: Gidan Dabino Publishers,100 Edition, February 2001.

Madauci, Ibrahim, Isa, Yahaya and Daura, Bello. *Hausa Customs*. Zaria: NNPC, 1968.

Maikaba, Balarabe. "Cinematic Conventions and the Influence of Western (Hollywood) and Indian (Bollywood) Cinema on Contemporary Hausa Home Video Drama." In *Hausa Home Videos: Technology, Economy and* Society. Eds. Abdalla Uba Adamu, Yusuf M. Adamu and Umar Faruk Jibrin. Kano: Centre for Hausa Cultural Studies, 2004, p. 100-105.

Mahmud, M. (2008). *Nigeria: Kannywood-Why They Must Be Censored*. Daily Trust, online edition https://allafrica.com/stories/200804290626.html.

Maiwada, D.A. "Imitation of Violence in Hausa Video Films and Consequences on Youth Behavior." In *Hausa Home Videos: Technology, Economy and Society*. Eds. Abdalla Uba Adamu, Yusuf M. Adamu. And Umar Faruk Jibrin. Kano: Centre for Hausa Cultural Studies, 2004. p, 272-275

Malumfashi, Ibrahim. *Adabin Kasuwar Kano*. Kano: Nasiha, 1994.

Malumfashi, Ibrahim. *Mene ne Adabin kasuwa*? Posted in the internet in 2013.

Manvell, Roger. *Theatre and Film: A Comparative Study of the Two Forms of Dramatic Art, and of the Problems of Adaptation of Stage Plays into Films*. London: Associated University Presses, Inc, 1979.

McCain, Carmen R. "Video Expose: Metafiction and Message in Nigerian Films" In *Journal of African Cinemas*. Volume 4 number 1, 2012, p. 25-57.

McCain, Carmen R. *The Politics of Exposure: Contested Cosmopolitanisms, Revelation of Secrets and Intermedial Reflexivity in Hausa Popular Expression.* Unpublished PhD Dissertation Submitted to University of Wisconsin-Madison, 2014, 420 pages.

Mckienan, D. W. *Cinema and Community.* London: Palgrave Macmillan. 2008.

Metz, Christian. *Film Language*: *A Semiotics of the Cinema.* New York: Oxford University Press. 1974.

Mohammed, Binta S. "Male Chauvinism: A Major Factor in the Manifestation of Sexism in Hausa Home Videos/Hausa video films." In *Hausa Home Videos/Hausa video films: Technology, Economy and Society.* Eds. Abdalla Uba Adamu, Yusuf M. Adamu and Umar Faruk Jibrin. Kano: Centre for Hausa Cultural Studies, 2004, p. 171- 176.

Mohammed, Hadiza Alfa. "Women on Screen: The Burning Issues. A Critical Appraisal on Women Acting in Nigeria Hausa Home Video." In *Hausa Home Video: Technology, Economy and Society.* Eds. Abdalla Uba Adamu, Yusuf M. Adamu and Umar Faruk Jibrin. Kano: Centre for Hausa Cultural Studies, 2004, p. 194-198.

Monaco, James. *How to Read A Film.* New York: Oxford University Press, 2000.

Muhammad, Nafisa Adamu. *Mata A Cikin Finafinan Hausa 1995-2002.* Unpublished MA Dissertation Submitted to the Department of Nigerian Languages. Kano: Bayero University, 2002, 205 pages.

Munia, Farahmeen. *Adaptation of Fairy Tales into Films: A Study of Two Disney Movies: Cinderela* (2015) and *Beauty and the Beast* (2017). An MA Thesis submitted to the Department of English and Humanities, Brac University. 2017. 30 pages.

Munkaila, Mohammed M. and Idoko, E.F. "Hausa Video Films and the Globalization Process." In *Maiduguri Journal of Linguistics and Literary Studies.* Volume VI. Maiduguri: University of Maiduguri, 2004, p. 54- 65.

Nagib, Lucia. "Ouedraogo and the Aesthetics of Silence." In. *African Oral Literature: Functions in Contemporary Contexts.* Ed. Kaschula Rusell. Cape Town: New Africa Education (NAE). 2001, p. 100-110.

Naremore, James. "Introduction: Film and the Reign of Adaptation" In *Film Analysis.* Ed. James Naremore. London: The Athlone Press, 2000, p. 1 – 15.

Njogu Kimani. *Media and Identity in Africa.* Edinburgh University Press, 2009.

Oha, Obododimma. "The Rhetoric of Nigerian Christian Videos: The War Paradigm of the Great Mistake." In *Nigerian Video Films.* Ed. Jonathan Haynes. Ohio: University Centre for International Studies, 2000, p. 192-199.

Okome, Onookome. "Women, Religion and the Video Film in Nigeria." In *Theatre, Performance and New Media in Africa.* Eds. Susan Arndt et al. Bayreuth: Bayreuth African Studies, 2007, p. 161-185.

Okpewho, Isidore. "Introduction: The Study of Performance." In *The Oral Performance in Africa.* Ed. Isidore Okpewho. Ibadan: Spectrum Books Limited. 1990, p. 1-20.

Okuyade, Ogaga. "Introduction: Familiar Realities, Continuity, and Shifts of Trajectory in the New African Novel." In *Tradition and Change in Contemporary West and East African Fiction.* Ed. Ogaga Okuyade. Amsterdam-New York: Rodopi. 2014, p. ix-xxxii.

Ong, Walter J. *Orality and Literacy: The Technologizing of the World.* London: Routledge, 1982.

Osofisan, Femi. "Yorùba Theatre in Crisis: Death or Transition?" In *Interfaces between the Oral and the Written: Versions and Subversions in African Literatures 2.* Eds. Alain Ricard & Flora Veit-Wild. Amsterdam: Rodopi, 2005, p. 181-199.

O''Siochru, Sean. *Social Consequences of the Globalization of the Media and Communication Sector: Some Strategic Considerations.* Geneva: International Labor Organization. 2004.

Peräkylä, Anssi. "Conversation Analysis." In *Qualitative Research Practice*. Eds. Seale Clive et al. Sage Publications, London, 2004, p. 165-179.

Peterson, Mark Allen. "From Jinn to Genies: Intertextuality, Media, and the Making of Global Folklore" In Sharon R. Sherman and Mikel J. Koven. Eds. *Folklore / Cinema: Popular Film as Vernacular Culture*. Utah: Utah State University Press, 2007. p. 93-112.

Petty, Sheila. "Postcolonial Geographies: Landscape and Alienation in *Clando*." In. *Cinema and Social Discourse in Cameroon*. Ed. Alexie Tcheuyap. Bayreuth: African Studies . 2005, p. 159-171.

Pfaff, Françoise. Ed. *Focus on African Films*. Bloomington: Indiana University Press, 2004.

Phillips, Patrick. *Understanding Film Texts*: *Meaning and Experience*. London: British Film Institute, 2000.

Piault, Colette. "Some Thoughts on Verbal and Non-verbal Expressions in Anthropological Films: Evolution, Techniques, Strategies, Problems." In *Oral Tradition and Its Transmission*: *The Many Forms of* Message. Eds. Siemaert Edgard et al. Durban: The Campbell Collections and Centre for Oral Studies. 1994, p. 1-11.

Pilaszewicz, Stanislaw. "Literature in the Hausa Language" in B. W. Andrzejewski *et al* (eds). *Literatures in African Languages*: *Theoretical Issues and Sample Surveys*. Cambridge: Cambridge University Press. 1985, p. 190-250.

Raw, Laurence and Gurr, Tony. "Bridging the Translation/Adaptation Divide: A Pedagogical View" In *Translation and Adaptation in Theatre and Film*. Ed. Katja Krebs. London: Routledge, 2014, p. 162 – 177.

Ricard, Alain & Veit-Wild, Flora. Eds. *Interfaces between the Oral and the Written: Versions and Subversions in African Literatures 2*. Amsterdam: Rodopi, 2005.

Robinson, C. H. *Specimens of Hausa Literature*. London: Cambridge University Press, 1896.

Roscoe, Adrian A. *Mother is Gold: A Study in West African Literature*. London: Cambridge University Press, 1971.

Rosenbaum, Jonathan. "Two Forms of Adaptation: *Housekeeping* and *Naked Lunch*" In *Film Adaptation*. Ed. James Naremore. London: The Athlone Press, 2000, p. 216 - 220

Rubin, Don. *The World Encyclopedia of Contemporary Theatre* London, New York: Routledge 1994.

Salawu, Abiodun. *Indigenous Language Media in Africa*. Lagos: Centre for Black and African Arts and Civilization (CBAAC), 2006.

Santos, Constantine. *The Epic Films of David Lean.* Lanham: The Scare crow Press, INC. 2012.

Schechner, Richard. "Victor Turner's Last Adventure", preface to Victor Turner, *The Anthropology of Performance.* New York: Performing Arts Journal Press, 1987, p. 7-20.

Schechner, Richard. *Performance Theory.* London and New York: Routledge Classics, 1988.

Scholz, Anne-Marie. *From Fidelity to History: Film Adaptations as Cultural Events in The Twentieth Century.* New York – Oxford: Berghahn, 2013.

Silverman, David. *Interpreting Qualitative Data: Methods for Analysing Talk, Text and Interaction.* Second Edition. London: Sage Publications, 2001.

Skinner, Neil. *An Anthology of Hausa Literature.* Zaria: NNPC, 1980.

Soyinka, Wole. "Forward: African Theatre: From *Ali Baba* to *Woza Albert*" In Don Rubin (ed). *The World Encyclopedia of Contemporary Theatre Volume 3 Africa.* London and New York: Routledge. 1997, p. 11-13.

Stam, Robert. "Beyond Fidelity: The Dialogics of Adaptation" In *Film Adaptation.* Ed. James Naremore. London: The Athlone Press, 2000, p. 54 – 76.

Sue, Engineer. *Longman Dictionary of Contemporary English*. London: Longman Group Ltd. 1978.

Sullivan, Joanna. "Exploring Bori as a Site of Myth in Hausa Culture". *Journal of African Culture,* vol 17 issue 2, 2005, p. 271-282.

Thackway, Melissa. *Africa Shoots Back: Alternative Perspectives in Sub-Saharan Francophone African Film*. Bloomington: Indiana University Press, 2003.

Tsika, Noah A. *Nollywood Stars: Media and Migration in West Africa and the Diaspora*. Bloomington: Indiana University Press, 2015.

Turner, Victor. *From Ritual to Theatre: The Human Seriousness of Play*. New York: PAJ Publications, 1982.

Turner, Victor. *The Anthropology of Performance*. New York: PAJ Publications, 1987.

Ukadike, N. Frank. *"Yeelen* (1987), Souleymane Cisse". In: Geiger, Jeffrey and Rutsky, R. L. Eds. *Film Analysis: A Norton Reader. Second Edition*. New York: W. W. Norton and Company, 2013, p. 756-775.

Umar, Adamu Aliyu. *Gudummawar Finafinan Zamani A Bangaren Adabin Hausa*. Unpublished BA Dissertation Submitted to the Department of Nigerian Languages. Kano: Bayero University, 2002, 114 pages.

Umar, Muhammad Balarabe. *Wasannin Tashe*. Zaria: NNPC, 1981.

Usman, Abdullahi Maikano. "Hana Fim a Kano Ba Adalci Ba Ne" In Yusuf Aliyu Lawan Gwazaye (Ed). *Muntaz*. Kano: Gidan Dabino Publishers. 100 Edition. February 2001, p. 13.

Usman, Bukar. *Taskar Tatsuniyoyi: Littafi Na Daya Zuwa Na Goma Sha Biyu*. Kano: Gidan Dabino Publishes, 2012.

Vetinde, Lifongo. "Reels of Conflicting Paradigms: The Black Filmmaker and the Africa"s Transitional Dilemmas" In Collier, Gordon (Ed). *Focus on Nigeria: Literature and Culture*. Amsterdam-New York: Rodopi. 2012, p. 457-488.

Wilkerson, James and Parkin Robert. "Modalities of Change: The Interface of Tradition and Modernity in East Asia" In James Wilkerson and Robert Parkin (Eds). *Modalities of Change: The Interface of Tradition and Modernity in East Asia*. New York: Berghahn Books. 2013, p. 1-20.

Wynchank, Anny. "The Cineaste as a Modern Griot in West Africa" In Siemart, Edgart, Cowper-Lewis and Bell, Nigel (Eds). *Oral Tradition and Its Transmission*: *The Many Forms of Message*. Durban: The Campbell Collections and Centre for Oral Studies. 1994, p. 12-26.

Yahaya, Ibrahim Yaro. *Hausa A Rubuce: Tarihin Rubuce-rubuce Cikin Hausa.* Zaria: NNPC, 1988.

Yahaya, Ibrahim Yaro. *Tatsuniyoyi Da Wassanni: Littafi Na Shid*a. Ibadan: Oxford University Press, 1971.

African Languages – African Literatures / Langues Africaines – Littératures Africaines

Frédérique Toudoire-Surlapierre; Ethmane Sall (éd.)
Les Francophonies « noires »
Histoire, mémoire, couleur, culture et identité
Cet ouvrage fait suite au colloque *Les Francophonies « noires »* qui s'est tenu les 26 et 27 janvier 2017 à l'Université de Haute-Alsace. Trois axes principaux structurent ce volume. C'est d'abord la « poétique des langues » qui est interrogée, selon une double perspective imaginaire et pragmatique, dans les contributions de P. Boizette, P. Fandio, J.-M. Devésa, B. Urbani et J. Serghini. V. Mendou, M. Anagonou et E. Sall posent ensuite la question du rapport (problématique) entre couleur et identité. Enfin, c'est en termes de stratégie que la couleur est pensée, autour des concepts de *storytelling*, d'appartenance et d'esthétisation.
Bd. 8, 2018, 278 S., 34,90 €, br., ISBN 978-3-643-91013-4

Priscillia M. Manjoh
Representations and Renegotiations of the Nation in Anglophone Cameroonian Literature
Bd. 7, 2018, 448 S., 44,90 €, br., ISBN 978-3-643-90891-9

Lindy Stiebel; Therese Steffen (Eds.)
Letters to my Native Soil
Lewis Nkosi writes home (2001 – 2009)
Bd. 6, 2014, 296 S., 34,90 €, br., ISBN 978-3-643-90510-9

Eshete Gemeda
African Egalitarian Values and Indigenous Genres
A Comparative Approach to the Functional and Contextual Studies of Oromo National Literature in a Contemporary Perspective
Bd. 5, 2012, 352 S., 34,90 €, br., ISBN 978-3-643-90233-7

Julie Cairnie; Dobrota Pucherova (Eds.)
Moving Spirit
The Legacy of Dambudzo Marechera in the 21st Century
Bd. 4. 2012. 216 S., 29,90 €, br., ISBN 978-3-643-90215-3

Edward O. Ako (Ed.)
Cameroon Literature in English
Critical Essays on Fiction and Drama
vol. 3, 2009, 256 pp., 29,90 €, br., ISBN 3-643-10192-1

Wumi Raji
Long Dreams in Short Chapters
Essays in African Postcolonial Literary, Cultural and Political Criticisms
vol. 2, 2009, 176 pp., 29,90 €, br., ISBN 978-3-8258-1841-8

Herbert Igboanusi
A Dictionary of Nigerian English Usage
vol. 1, 2010, 384 pp., 19,90 €, br., ISBN 978-3-8258-1453-3

Sahara-Studien / Sahara Studies / Études sahariennes
hrsg. von / edited by / éditées par Dr. habil. Tilman Musch (Universität Bayreuth)

Musch, Tilman Mahama Abalaiyi Sediké

Dāga Tudaa – Pensées Toubou
Proverbes du Sahara Central
Bd. 1, 2021, 306 S., 39,90 €, br., ISBN 978-3-643-25065-0

LIT Verlag Berlin – Münster – Wien – Zürich – London
Auslieferung Deutschland / Österreich / Schweiz: siehe Impressumsseite

Beiträge zur Afrikaforschung

hrsg. vom Institut für Afrika-Studien der Universität Bayreuth

Emmanuel Sackey
Dynamic Tensions, Civil Society and Development of the Disability Rights Movement
Bd. 95, 2019, 256 S., 34,90 €, br., ISBN 978-3-643-91087-5

Umar Ahmed
Gender in Media Discourse
The Discursive Construction of Gender in Nigerian Newspapers
Bd. 94, 2019, 244 S., 29,90 €, br., ISBN 978-3-643-91085-1

Issifou Abou Moumouni
Gouvernance de la sécurité au Bénin
Les chasseurs néo-traditionnels dans le système sécuritaire
Bd. 93, 2019, 282 S., 39,90 €, br., ISBN 978-3-643-14195-8

Carline Liliane Ngawa Mbaho
La vente de produits de santé dans les cars interurbains au Cameroun
Une analyse interactionnelle
Bd. 92, 2018, 304 S., 39,90 €, br., ISBN 978-3-643-14163-7

Georg Materna
Straßenhandel mit Souvenirs im Senegal
Akteure, Arbeit und Organisation
Bd. 91, 2020, 446 S., 54,90 €, br., ISBN 978-3-643-14128-6

Mulugeta Bezabih Mekonnen
Transnational Migration-Development Nexus
The Engagement of Ethiopian Diaspora Associations Based in Germany
Bd. 90, 2018, 374 S., 44,90 €, br., ISBN 978-3-643-91028-8

Christian Ungruhe
Lasten tragen, Moderne befördern
Wanderarbeit, Jugend, Erwachsenwerden und ihre geschlechtsspezifischen Differenzierungen in Ghana
Bd. 89, 2018, 456 S., 54,90 €, br., ISBN 978-3-643-14011-1

Tamer M.A. Abd Elkreem
Power Relations of Development
The Case of Dam Construction in the Nubian Homeland, Sudan
Bd. 88, 2018, 426 S., 34,90 €, br., ISBN 978-3-643-91008-0

Stephan Bock
Translations of Urban Regulation in Relations between Kigali (Rwanda) and Singapore
Bd. 87, 2018, 358 S., 44,90 €, br., ISBN 978-3-643-90986-2

Justice Anquandah Arthur
The Politics of Religious Sound
Conflict and the Negotiation of Religious Diversity in Ghana
Bd. 86, 2018, 358 S., 39,90 €, br., ISBN 978-3-643-90982-4

Jean Pierre Boutché
Fula spoken in the City of Maroua (Northern Cameroon)
A sociolinguistic insight into its use by non-ethnic speakers
Bd. 85, 2020, 340 S., 44,90 €, br., ISBN 978-3-643-90974-9

LIT Verlag Berlin – Münster – Wien – Zürich – London
Auslieferung Deutschland / Österreich / Schweiz: siehe Impressumsseite